THE AFRICAN AMERICAN STUDENT'S GUIDE TO SURVIVING GRADUATE SCHOOL

Graduate Survival Skills

Series Editor

Bruce A. Thyer, Ph.D.
Research Professor of Social Work
University of Georgia

The volumes in this series attempt to demystify the process of earning a graduate degree. They seek to meet the need among young scholars for insights into the workings of graduate schools, from the application and admissions process through finding an academic job.

This series is targeted at readers interested in strategies for improving their experience in and with graduate school. The authors of the books come from a variety of academic disciplines, and a variety of career stages. Volumes in the series thus far include:

We invite ideas for future books in this series. Possible topics include:

Getting Into Graduate School, Financing Your Graduate Education, Completing Your Dissertation or Thesis, Working With Your Major Professor or Advisory Committee, Maintaining a Rewarding Personal Life as a Graduate Student, and *Handling Difficult or Sensitive Situations While in Graduate School.*

We encourage authors from all academic disciplines, and at any career stage. Potential authors can submit formal proposals (along with a current c.v.) for individual titles to the Series Editor.

THE AFRICAN AMERICAN STUDENT'S GUIDE TO SURVIVING GRADUATE SCHOOL

Alicia Isaac

GRADUATE SURVIVAL SKILLS

SAGE Publications
International Educational and Professional Publisher
Thousand Oaks   London   New Delhi

For information address:

SAGE Publications, Inc.
2455 Teller Road
Thousand Oaks, California 91320
E-mail: order@sagepub.com

SAGE Publications Ltd.
6 Bonhill Street
London EC2A 4PU
United Kingdom

SAGE Publications India Pvt. Ltd.
M-32 Market
Greater Kailash I
New Delhi 110 048 India

Printed in the United States of America

Library of Congress Cataloging-in-Publication Data

Isaac, Alicia.
     The African American student's guide to surviving graduate school/
by Alicia Isaac.
          p.   cm. — (Graduate survival skills; v. 5)
     Includes bibliographical references and index.
     ISBN 0-7619-0381-X (cloth: acid-free paper).
     ISBN 0-7619-0382-8 (pbk.: acid-free paper)
     1. Afro-American—Education (Graduate).   2. Afro-American graduate
students.   I. Title.   II. Series.
     LC2781.7.I83   1998
     378.1'55—dc21   97-45381

This book is printed on acid-free paper.

98 99 00 01 02 03 10 9 8 7 6 5 4 3 2 1

Acquiring Editor:	Jim Nageotte
Editorial Assistant:	Fiona Lyon
Production Editor:	Denise Santoyo
Production Assistant:	Michèle Lingre
Book Designer/Typesetter:	Janelle LeMaster

This book is dedicated to my mother, *Joan Parler Isaac*, and every African American woman instilling in us the desire to meet the challenge. I love you all.

———————•———————

An African American Graduate Student's Creed

I am. I can. I did. The strength and beauty of who I am will never be unknown to me again.
—Alicia R. Isaac

No matter what, just try your best.
—Ashley Pari Green, Age 7

CONTENTS

SERIES EDITOR'S INTRODUCTION

From the initial conceptualization of this series on *Surviving Graduate School,* a volume devoted to African American students was seen as an essential contribution. I was most fortunate to recruit a very talented faculty member, Alicia Isaac, DPA, to prepare this book, *The African American Student's Guide to Surviving Graduate School.* Although she has been a faculty member since 1989, Dr. Isaac received her doctorate in public administration just 2 years ago, so she is keenly sensitive to contemporary issues facing black graduate students who must balance the concurrent demands of academics, earning an income, supporting a family, and maintaining a personal life.

In some respects, for African American graduate students it is both the best of times and the worst of times. Opportunities abound for graduate study in a variety of fields, and financial aid is often available to help support one's studies. Most universities are making conscientious attempts to proactively recruit and retain talented graduate students of color, and to make the campus environment more accepting and friendlier for students of diverse backgrounds. Nevertheless, long-established affirmative action programs are under constant attack, legally and otherwise, and in some academic and professional fields black graduate student enrollment has recently dropped as a consequence.

Despite these trends, the situation remains fairly positive. The talented African American student who applies to several graduate programs is highly likely to be accepted by at least one. The prospects of receiving some form of financial assistance are good, particularly for the proactive student. Once admitted, you are to some extent on your own, but the job prospects for African Americans with graduate or professional degrees are excellent in most fields. The obstacles are many, but the rewards can be great.

Dr. Alicia R. Isaac's guidebook provides valuable advice on managing one's life as a graduate student, lessons she has acquired personally through her broad array of social and professional contacts within academia and through scholarly study of the university milieu. I believe that you will find this volume to be a marvelous help for yourself, for friends and family members who are contemplating enrollment, or who are currently enrolled in graduate school. It would also make a terrific inspirational gift for the student completing an undergraduate degree! Enjoy.

—BRUCE A. THYER
Series Editor

PREFACE

I was greatly inspired by a book that I have read and reread many times, *The Instant Millionaire* by Mark Fisher (1991). The book imprinted two important principles on my consciousness, which I fervently live by each day. First, anything can be accomplished. Second, there is a scientific process for accomplishing goals and dreams with ease if we learn the process and practice it diligently.

When I was pursuing my master's and doctorate degrees, I didn't know the principles or have a clue about what the scientific process was. I just took bits and pieces of information that I heard or read and went with the flow. This game plan worked well in my master's program, but it caused me a great deal of anxiety and stress in my doctoral program. Basically, I didn't know exactly what to do. I had very wonderful people giving me guidance here and there on specific parts of the process, but no one sat me down and said, "This is what you do."

My mission in writing this book is to say to you, "This is what you do." I've tried to say it as straightforwardly as possible in a way that appeals to your intellect and your emotions. This is not just an academic experience, but a human one as well. I hope the words on these pages inspire you to "run the race without ceasing, and get to the finish line in grand style." The world needs us.

Acknowledgments

A heartfelt and special thanks

To all my friends and colleagues who contributed information, good cheer, and support and who made writing this book a wonderful experience:

Especially: Rev. Carmen Young, Dr. Agnes Green, Dr. Lettie Lockhart, Robert Brandau, Cedric Masten, and Velma Mustakeem.

To all the contributors who added their stories or coauthored chapters.

To my parents, my brother, and Ashley and Joshua (the generation to come).

Finally, to my friend, advisor, and editor, Dr. Bruce Thyer, and Jim Nageotte and all of the folks at Sage Publications.

1

GRADUATE SCHOOL IS . . .

WHAT IS GRADUATE SCHOOL?

Graduate school is an established institution through which one receives an advanced degree. In this case, *institution* means more than the actual place—the college or university where one receives the degree. Graduate school is the place, the process, and the interaction with people encountered during the receipt of higher academic learning. It is the place to receive advanced credentials and skills required to be considered prepared and well-educated in the adult world.

Graduate school may be described in several ways. Some of the most common descriptors are challenging, confusing, scary, exhilarating, taxing, inspiring, humiliating, and rewarding. Graduate school is significantly different from undergraduate studies because graduate students are expected to think independently, postulate theories, and be able to test hypotheses with a more limited amount of structure and guidance than that of undergraduates. Master's level students are expected to be able to operationalize and evaluate knowledge, whereas doctoral candidates are expected to be contributors to that knowledge.

By all accounts, though graduate school may be a wonderful experience, it is also hard. It takes vast amounts of time, energy, and money. In addition, it takes skill. The most successful students have adequate preparation, political savvy, common sense, good networking and resource development techniques, written and oral communication skills, and a sense of purpose.

African American students report that all of these required attributes are necessary for them to an even greater extent than for their white colleagues. Many are first-generation graduate scholars. Others are juggling significant financial worries to attend graduate school. Most study for degrees at predominantly white institutions, because there are only a few historically black colleges and universities with graduate programs. Besides the rigors of academia, graduate school requires a significant cultural and philosophical adjustment for them.

African American undergraduates, current graduate students, and those considering graduate school have many dilemmas, maybe even more than white students, due to their personal and racial histories and the economic and political structures in the United States and the world. Their decisions and contemplations must be more critical if they are to have an impact on their own lives and the lives of others. In many ways, African American generations have emerged knowing or being told that there is an important agenda that must be tended to, and it will be those with advanced knowledge and skills who must be the masterminds.

Not all the deliberations about becoming an advanced scholar have to do with a contribution to the greater good of society. Some delierations about graduate school are purely individualistic and purposefully centered on attaining wealth, power, prestige, or a satisfying career. These are all very important reasons for attending graduate school, and the context in which they are explored evokes a great deal of thought.

The deliberations about graduate school contribute many of the philosophical questions many African Americans often contemplate about attending graduate school:

- Should I select a field that I really dream about and can be passionate about, or should I select a field that has more income potential, though I have less passion for it?
- How can I be sure that graduate school is really the credential that I need for accomplishing my life goals?
- Am I giving up a piece of who I am by subscribing to the idea that my worth and opportunities may be greatly enhanced by emulating a process used by majority cultures? Am I gaining a piece of who I am by preparing myself as best I can to be competitive in a society or world that may not be fair or equitable?
- What will be expected of me as an advanced scholar? Will I be obligated to make a contribution to the greater good of society?

Suppose I don't want to bear the burden of effecting change just because I have received an advanced education?

* Is graduate school worth all of the challenges, frustration, possible humiliation, and constant tests to my self-esteem? Not everyone wins, not everyone finishes; what is in store for me?

After exploring and attempting to answer these and other questions, while weighing the benefits versus the colsts most African Americans would say that the benefits of graduate school far outweigh the costs, but it takes courage, dedication, determination, and many other qualities to succeed. In other words, it's worth the struggle.

THE MASTER'S DEGREE

The master's degree is the advanced degree between the baccalaureate and the PhD. There are more than 200 different master's degrees, and approximately 300,000 master's degrees are awarded each year. In some fields, the master's degree is considered the terminal degree and is not considered the stepping-stone to a doctorate. The Master's in Business Administration (MBA), Master's in Social Work (MSW), or Master's in Library Science (MLS) are examples of such degrees.

Master's programs for full-time study typically last from 1 to 2 years and usually consist of course work, some type of comprehensive exam, and a thesis or research project. A large number of master's students are engaged in part-time study.

THE DOCTORATE

The doctorate is the most prestigious of all diplomas and is the highest academic degree one can achieve. Besides the PhD (Doctor of Philosophy), there are approximately 30 other named doctorates, such as Doctor of Public Administration (DPA), Doctor of Education (EdD), Doctor of Psychology (PsyD), Doctor of Pharmacy (PharmD), or Doctor of Social Work (DSW). Compared to all of the other degrees, the doctorate is the most prized but the most challenging to receive.

Requirements for the doctorate include course work, written and oral comprehensive exams, the dissertation, and the dissertation defense.

THE NEED FOR AFRICAN AMERICANS
TO OBTAIN GRADUATE DEGREES

African Americans have a social and cultural obligation to obtain advanced degrees. It is necessary in today's society, considering the lack of equitable representation across all segments of society and the devaluation of the undergraduate degree. Almost all leadership and managerial positions in public or private industry require either professional or advanced degrees. It is estimated that by the year 2000 the bachelor's degree may be comparable to a high school diploma in many fields. For African Americans to compete, they must have the proper graduate credentials. Further, African Americans with graduate degrees must serve as role models and contribute to the knowledge base of industry, business, science, human services, the arts, and other fields.

Besides the need for African Americans to engage in graduate studies for leadership and cultural benefit, there is also an economic necessity for African Americans to have advanced degrees. According to the U.S. Department of Commerce, Bureau of the Census, in the United States the median annual income in 1993 of a man older than 25 with a doctorate degree was $63,149, compared with $42,757 for a man with a bachelor's degree. For a woman with a doctorate in the same year, the median annual income was $47,248 compared with $31,197 for a woman with a bachelor's degree. A similar disparity shows the median annual income of men with master's degrees at $51,867, $9,110 more than with bachelor's degrees. The disparity for women in the same categories was $7,415.

Unemployment statistics in 1994 indicate that the unemployment rate for African Americans 25 years old and older with a bachelor's or higher degree was only 3.5%. This was significantly lower than for African Americans without the college credential, at over 10%.

THE CURRENT LANDSCAPE OF
AFRICAN AMERICANS IN GRADUATE SCHOOLS

The Digest of Education Statistics (National Center for Education Statistics, 1995) reports that in the fall of 1976, the total number of students *enrolled* in graduate school was 1,322,500. The total number of African American graduate students was 78,500—32,000 men and 46,500 women.

From fall 1993, the total number of students enrolled in graduate school was 1,689,300. The total number of African American graduate students was 101,700; 35,100 men and 66,600 women. In 1993, African Americans accounted for only 6.02% of all graduate students in the United States. Also, the number of African Americans in graduate schools in 1993 made up less than 1% of the entire African American population in the United States (National Center for Education Statistics, 1995).

In 1992 to 1993, 368,701 master's degrees were conferred by institutions of higher education in the United States. Master's degrees were granted to 19,780 African Americans; 12,959 women and 6,821 men. Of all master's degrees awarded in this country, only 5% went to African Americans. Business management and administrative services and education were the two top fields for African American men, whereas ROTC and military technologies and foreign languages and literature were the lowest. The two top fields for black women receiving master's degrees were education, business management and administrative services. The smallest numbers granted to women were in ROTC and communications technologies (National Center for Education Statistics, 1995).

In 1992 to 1993, there were 42,021 doctorates awarded in the United States. Only 1,352, approximately 3% of all doctorates, went to African Americans. Of that total, 737 were women and 615 were men. The top five fields for African Americans were as follows: a) Education, b) Psychology, c) Theological studies, d) Social sciences and history, and e) Health professions and related sciences. The top five fields for whites receiving doctorates were a) Education, b) Psychology, c) Biological and life sciences, d) Physical sciences and science technologies, and e) Engineering (National Center for Education Statistics, 1995).

THE URGENCY FOR AFRICAN AMERICANS TO OBTAIN GRADUATE DEGREES

Clearly, African Americans are underrepresented in graduate school at the master's and doctoral levels. We know that this is a disadvantage because a larger pool of qualified African American candidates gives us more leverage to compete in a highly competitive market. Corporations and public institutions continue to say that they wish there were more African American candidates to consider when searching to fill high-level positions. Although this may be rhetoric, it will take larger numbers of well-qualified candidates available for selection to eliminate this as an excuse.

Earlier in the chapter, there was a list of contemplative questions that every African American should sit down and formally consider as he or she makes decisions about graduate school. These are important and should not be taken lightly. Though this book will not make up your mind for you about a graduate degree, consider the following points:

1. If you can go to graduate school, you should. Our society and culture needs your expertise. Don't fall into the trap of "working first" and going back later. Later may never come, and in most cases it is much harder when it does. I almost always advise African American students to get the master's or doctorate first and worry about work experience afterward.

2. Graduate degrees are better financial investments than most undergraduate degrees. The years put into study can substantially increase your earning power over the years. The lure of money, a new car, and other material possessions immediately after receiving a bachelor's degree are usually gold-plated instead of real gold. With devalued salaries, one's money does not go nearly as far as new graduates think.

3. African Americans, individually and as a culture, can benefit from having advanced credentials. Typically, Dr. Jones still earns a lot more respect than Mr. Jones ever did.

REAL STORIES

The following stories reflect the accounts of actual African American graduate school survivors. Their stories are different, because they are different people in different places, under different circumstances. But, you will see many parallels to experiences of other graduate students, and several important themes run through their stories and the stories of almost all African American graduate scholars.

Cedric's Story

I was worried, because black students in many predominantly white institutions have been made to feel inferior because of some twisted view of affirmative action and the knowledge that they were admitted under special admissions circumstances as a result of academic deficiencies. This happened to many of my friends and it added an "undue burden," because they were in constant fear that someone would bring it up, and it *was* often brought up. Further, they know that they were never seen as equally competent by professors or peers.

Personally, I was challenged with making a crucial decision about graduate school shortly after completing a rigorous 4-year baccalaureate program in psychology and special education. Though the decision included many complex issues, it was one that I knew had to be made because of what I saw as the decreasing value of a bachelor's degree.

Prior to enrolling in a graduate psychology program, I spent a great deal of time working through fear. The fear of failing created a significant amount of anxiety, as I frequently felt inadequate or that I did not deserve to embark on a promising career as a psychotherapist. Additionally, taking the Graduate Record Examination, writing a statement of purpose, and filling out the graduate application was intimidating and almost overwhelming. To combat the fear, I told myself over and over that I could do graduate school.

Once past the fear, I was able to develop a keen sense of my strengths and weaknesses as they related to what schools were looking for. This process of self-evaluation allowed me to deal with the admissions requirements one step at a time. Fortunately, I was admitted to the graduate school of my choice, but I had no earthly idea how this endeavor would be financed. I had several credit card balances, a new car, and a $40,000 undergraduate diploma to pay for.

My immediate mission became how to get the money to cover the first year of graduate school. I figured with an extreme "bare bones budget," I could do it with $18,000. Three ideas came to me: selling M&M candies, sending letters to 100 organizations, and offering a term paper assistance service.

With the help of 20 fraternity brothers, 200 cases of candy were sold in 4 weeks, yielding a profit of $2,000. During the same period, 12 of the 100 organizations I had written to encouraged me to submit transcripts, writing samples, and essays to their scholarship committees. To my surprise, checks totaling $16,000 came in from the NAACP, Minorities in Action Committee, African Men Move Inc., and other sources! The term paper assistance business earned another $1,400 before I gave it up. *Two weeks prior to entering graduate school, I politely declined the Financial Aid Office's offer of $18,000 in student loans!*

After enrolling as a graduate student, I spent the first 3 weeks literally in chaos and confusion. I was faced with rigid deadlines and did not understand the tangential pontifications of my professors. Fearing that I would get the "stupid look" from my peers, I avoided asking questions. Three weeks later, I haphazardly stumbled across the only African American professor on campus. To my surprise, she greeted me and congratulated me on my endeavor—being admitted to graduate school.

A wonderful mentoring relationship developed over time. During our weekly meetings, I embraced the harsh feedback as it related to my research papers, and I was challenged to analyze information critically as opposed to writing facts, I also grew interpersonally, as I realized that giving back to the community was a necessity and not an option. Because I understood my purpose, I had no time to stand around fearing the challenge. Questions were asked and answers were demanded. Goals were set and the deadlines met.

Proudly, I can say that I completed the master's degree and now, several years later, I hope to complete my doctoral comprehensive exams very soon. So, to all African American men who have the dream, know that you can do it. For those without a dream, get one!

Joan's Story

It had always been my dream to get a master's in business and teach in a community college setting. I had anticipated being much younger when I started this endeavor, but raising a family and making a significant contribution to the financial stability of the family took precedent. Once my children were in college, I decided to return to school and work on my master's degree. I attended a historically black university at night while continuing to work during the day.

I made many sacrifices to obtain my Master's in Business Education, ranging from having to give up family and relaxation time, to having to drive 30 miles each way to school and back after having worked all day. Nevertheless, the struggle was worth it. Not only was I able to reach my academic dreams, but I had many enriching experiences along the way. I met wonderful friends who became study partners and colleagues in the program, because they were all the same major and took the same classes. The environment was stimulating and exciting. There was a significant amount of reading and studying and exams were hard. Nevertheless, learning was fun and graduate school opened a new door for me.

Alicia's Story

Looking back on my graduate school career, I had the opportunity to be an accomplished scholar very early on. However, I made some poor choices that impeded my progress but made me a stronger person and taught me some very valuable lessons.

I think that at some point in my life I had the potential to be a genius, but the gift in me was never fully developed. I talked and mastered motor skills at a very early age, and I learned to read at age three. I zoomed through school making all "As," never really having to study. It was as if I had a photographic memory, and the ability to do abstract and analytical thinking was a normal process. I finished high school early, went to college at 16, and entered a master's program at 19. Upon completion of the master's program 15 months later, I had my sights set on a doctoral program where I had been guaranteed admission.

As life sometimes makes turns that we are not fully cognizant of at the moment, I decided to get married instead of going on to doctoral studies, for no real reason that I can think of, looking back on it. Maybe it was just the novelty of being married or an immature decision made by a 21-year-old. The marriage was an abysmal failure, and the dream to receive a doctorate got buried until I realized that completing my dream was the path back to self-esteem and putting my life back together.

I entered a doctoral program bruised and reeling from a marriage gone wrong. Because I had not been smart in protecting my financial future, I had no money even though the marriage had generated money, which was still in my ex-husband's possession. All I had starting the program was a graduate assistantship provided by the university, a couple of supportive friends, and my determination.

Even though I already had a master's and had been successful in my field, I took a job at the local Winn-Dixie as a cashier so that I could have a "mindless job" that did not interfere with my schooling. I made it through one doctoral class after another, sometimes not even being able to afford my books. About midway through my course work I secured a job as adjunct faculty, teaching at night at a local college. There were days when I literally thought that I would not make it. But by the time I finished my course work, I had also been employed in a wonderful job in my field.

Completing a doctoral program while working was stressful at best. In addition to the personal problems surrounding my divorce and finances, I was at a predominantly white university with few supports that I could access. I didn't have time to meet in groups and have a mentor because I had to work. I survived my comprehensive and oral exams alone except for a few friends. I survived writing my dissertation and the most grueling single event of my life, the dissertation defense, with the help of a colleague, family, and a group of friends. The only thing that kept me from quitting was my determination. I had come too far to turn back.

Now that I've made it through, I must go back and help others along the path. Am I happy I did it? Unequivocally, yes. Do I still feel the pain? Yes. Would I recommend it? Yes, but only to students with open eyes, determination, and a plan for success.

IS GRADUATE SCHOOL WORTH IT?

The decision to attend graduate school is one of the most important you will ever make. You will have to search yourself and your past while getting in touch with what you see as your future. This self-reflection is the first step in the process. Everything else flows from your making a personal decision that graduate school is worth it.

2

MAKING THE RIGHT CHOICE ABOUT WHERE TO GO TO GRADUATE SCHOOL AND GETTING IN WITH MONEY

SELECTING THE RIGHT SCHOOL

One of the most critical decisions you need to make is which school to attend. Obviously, there are several personal and professional factors to consider. Do you want to go out-of-state? How much financial support is available? Who are the prominent experts in the field with whom you want to study? Of course, one of the most pivotal issues will be which schools accept you. Each of these individual factors comes together to determine the criteria you will use to select a graduate school.

There is no magical formula for selecting the right school. Nevertheless, there are some important indicators you can use as a guide. Look for what many professionals in the admissions business call "goodness of fit." Simply put, is the school right for you and are you right for the school? This "goodness of fit" appears academically, socially, emotionally, and economically. Here are some examples to illustrate the point.

• John's long-term dream is to be an administrator or CEO of a large, for profit psychological services company. John already has work experience and an undergraduate and master's degree in the behavioral sciences fields, but he has no experience or course work in management or administration. He is considering a doctorate in a community counseling field or a doctorate in a human services management field. What should he do? Because of the information given, John's best choice would be the doctorate in the human services management field or another administrative degree. Should John go for the doctorate or the second master's, such as the MBA? For an African American male, (or female, for that matter), "Dr." in front of the name intrinsically will be the better credential. One can always take other management courses later. John decided to pursue the PhD.

• Sowandé has long been in touch with her Afrocentrism, having grown up in a household that honors African, and African American history and fully practices the principles of Kwanzaa. She has worn her hair naturally since her birth and loves the bright, beautiful clothing that symbolizes the African heritage. She spends a great deal of time outdoors and loves the sun and the beach, having lived all of her life in California. She has been offered a substantial funding package to attend a predominantly white doctoral program in North Dakota for 4 years. She will be one of the two African American students in the entire graduate school, she is also being courted by several other schools. What should Sowandé do? She decided to look at other schools and ask the school in North Dakota for an extended period to make a decision. (Let's face it, they probably do not have a cadre of African American students making application, so she's got some leverage here. In reality, this offer does not look like a "goodness of fit" for Sowandé, though she may learn many valuable things.)

• Reggie met a graduate recruiter for a master's program and had a great conversation about the school. According to the recruiter, the school was prestigious, had an excellent academic program, had state-of-the-art technology and resources, great sports, African American fraternities and sororities, and many other outstanding qualities. When visiting the school, Reggie immediately noticed that the program within the school that he was applying to had no mentoring program, no African American faculty nor organized student groups, no computer support lab, no writing skills lab, and only a commitment from individual professors to assist students with difficulties. Because Reggie suffered from a learning disability, these areas were of major concern to him.

Although the school had many great qualities, Reggie decided that this was not a good match for him.

• Kelly received a substantial assistantship offer from a very prominent school in the Northeast to get a master's degree in genetics. It was one of the top three schools to which she applied. She researched the program, visited the campus, and talked to recent African American alumni. All of these experiences added up to a very positive picture of the school. This was not her number one choice based on prestige of the program and school, but the funding was better and she really liked the atmosphere of this school more. What should Kelly do? Kelly decided to go for the number two choice.

Tips for Selecting the Right Graduate School

• Start by determining your area of interest, and seek schools that match it as closely as possible. Be aware that not all schools will offer a degree or a degree program area in your field, but they may still offer a degree and course work that meet your career goals. So, don't rule out a program just because it does not offer a degree with the exact name that you are looking for. Nevertheless, it is important to evaluate the curriculum and the reputation of the school in the field.

• Evaluate the school's admission rate and attrition rate, and attempt to find out if they have an attrition policy. This is particularly important for African Americans, because it offers a view of how many black students get into a program and how many get out. An evaluation of the attrition policy gives insight into the efforts that a school will make to retain African American students. A school that graduates most of its African American students usually has the supports and other necessary resources available for students to succeed.

• Select a school that enhances the success of African American students. Such a school should have mentoring programs, computer supports, writing assistance, and other creative programs that allow individuals to maximize their strengths and learn new skills.

• If you need financial assistance, select the school that offers you a good funding package. Though funding should not be the only criterion, it is often the most important if there are no other monetary resources available. Often in my job as an admissions director, I would meet students who really had their hopes pinned on attending a particular school, but that school made no funding offer, whereas another one did. My question to them would be, "Can you attend graduate school without the money?" If the answer was yes, I would encourage them to consider their first choice if they could complete the program without significant student loan debt. If the answer was no or they would incur a student loan debt greater than $10,000 (including any undergraduate loans), I would encourage them to strongly consider the program offering the funding, if other important supports were in place.

• Explore the social milieu and the social supports, and decide if you can live with them. Graduate school is challenging, but you don't have to be miserable. Again, most students who do well have the right balance of academics and a rewarding personal life.

• Check the language requirements and other requirements specific to each program. Overall, you may not want to select a school that has a language requirement if that is not important to you or to your discipline.

• Be familiar with the prestige of the school. Though it may seem shallow, if you have a choice that will not enhance your long-term career goals, consider the school that may be most helpful in marketing yourself in the future.

• Don't get locked into a specific school or specific location mindset (if I can't go there, I won't go anywhere). Be open to the limitless possibilities. Some students may have the opportunity to attend any graduate school they wish. For others, owing to finances and logistics, the only choice may be the graduate school in their local area. This is okay, too. The important point here is that you obtain the graduate degree. For those who aren't accepted into the specific school applied to, there is still the opportunity to go to graduate school if you have the basic qualities. There *is* a graduate school somewhere that will take you if you are persistent enough.

How to Get Information About Graduate Schools

There are several ways to obtain information about graduate schools. Most college and university libraries and many large public libraries will have in their collections reference materials about graduate schools all over the world. These sources tend to be very comprehensive and provide a great deal of demographic information, such as the size of the student body, faculty ratio, and so forth. Many schools also have web pages that provide a great deal of helpful facts. This is a first step in listing schools to be explored. Here are a few of the most highly recommended library resources that are published yearly.

Peterson's Guides to Graduate and Professional Programs (Peterson's Guides, 1997)

The GRE/GCS Directory (published by the Educational Testing Service, Princeton, New Jersey)

The Chronicle of Higher Education (an educational periodical published by the American Association of University Professors)

Another way to obtain information is to contact the schools directly and ask that information be sent about the program and the school in general. Use the Internet, computer software programs on graduate school information, and visit schools' Websites. After reading the information you have, don't hesitate to ask for additional information and printed materials.

Consult other people who may have information about schools or graduate programs. Some of these people include professors, alumni, sorority sisters or fraternity brothers, family members, and friends. Some of the best insight comes from people who have firsthand information. If you are applying to a predominantly white college or university, ask the school for a list of addresses and telephone numbers of recent African American alumni. Call or write them and then ask them to give you the addresses and telephone numbers of some of their peers who were not on the list that the school gave you. Get in touch with them and ask candid questions about the school. By all means, make contact with African American faculty at the school. Speak with more than one to get the broadest range of information possible. Ask these people the tough questions and realistically evaluate their answers.

Once you have narrowed your list, visit the schools that you are really interested in. Visits may be costly, but they are worth the cost in relation to the information they yield. Getting a good feel for the program, campus, professors, and students may prevent a bad decision. Plan your visit so that you can meet several people, including administration, faculty, staff, and students. Talk to people individually and in groups. Spend time with students in various stages of the process, asking questions about courses, library research, study groups, and any other issues that interest or concern you.

The Final Decision

The decision of which graduate school to choose will be one of the most important you ever make. So you should make it with a great deal of information. Even with a significant amount of information, you will be confronted with other facets of the decision. For example, should you attend a historically black institution because of personal principles? Is it limiting to receive a doctorate from the same school where you received the master's? The jury is still out on these two questions. Research does not indicate that African Americans have been penalized by getting master's and doctorate from the same institution, though many would argue the contrary. And who would go on record as saying that a doctorate from Penn State is better than a doctorate from Howard? Some graduates from Penn State, maybe? You will have to make your own choices about these issues based on the information and perceptions you have. The most important thing is not to let the complexities of decisions about school selection keep you from attending graduate school somewhere.

ADMISSION TO GRADUATE SCHOOL

The Application Process

Applying to graduate schools is a manageable and stressless process if it is done scientifically. Once you have done the initial research and narrowed the selection of schools to apply to, you can organize the tasks and duplicate them for each school's application process. Many potential graduate scholars wonder how many schools should end up on the final list, and although there are no hard and fast numbers, most people should end with around three to five but no more than 10. How many schools to apply to should be dictated by the sincere interest in each program, the amount of money available to spend on application fees, postage, and copying, and the likelihood of an easy admission to a graduate program. Specifically, students with excellent grade point averages and GRE (Graduate Record Exam) scores will be more likely to be accepted by the schools they apply to, so they may choose to apply to fewer schools, whereas candidates with weaknesses in the application may have to shop around for more schools to get admitted. On the other hand, excellent candidates may also apply to many schools seeking to set up a wide range of funding offers.

The process usually entails obtaining the application materials; completing and returning the materials, including personal statement, résumé, and writing samples; having transcripts, test scores, and recommendations sent; and possibly an interview. Specifics will be provided by the school.

Preparing the Application Materials

The application process may take several months from start to completion, so start early. Set up a file specifically for each school that you intend to apply to. Any file system can be used; just make sure that there is a way to store documents that need to go out separately from your copies of those documents. Also, make sure there is a place to attach a checklist of application requirements that can be easily seen and updated each time a piece goes out or comes in. List the persons writing recommendations and when they received the recommendation forms. Keep these files as accurately as you would if you were an accountant managing a very important business portfolio.

Complete all forms in the application packet as accurately and honestly as possible. Have transcripts sent from the schools you have attended. Don't try to hide information, such as a bad math class at junior college; chances are, it will turn up on another transcript somewhere and look suspicious. Rather than trying to hide it, write a letter explaining the circumstances. If you don't understand a specific question, call the admissions office or a faculty contact for clarification. Type the forms or generate a computer application. Your application packet should be as aesthetically pleasing, but still appropriate, as you can make it. Having been an admissions director and having reviewed as many as 750 applications per year, I remember two kinds that stood out even before the first word was read: the ones that looked really good to the eye and the ones that looked really bad.

The personal narrative or statement of purpose should be well written and clearly related to the questions or topic areas requested by the school. The personal narrative should speak to the applicant's goals, strengths, and goodness of fit in the program, as well as illuminate the applicant's writing skills. Have a professor or another knowledgeable person read and edit the narrative for grammar, spelling, synthesis, and appropriateness of content. Center the personal narrative on specified themes, as opposed to writing a rambling chronology of your life experiences. Busy admissions committees do not have time to read statements that are not focused, and well written. A poorly written narrative may signal writing difficulties that will be problematic once an applicant matriculates in the graduate program. Typically when there are more applicants than spaces, and when test scores and grades are comparable, the quality of the personal narrative determines who gets in and who does not. The narrative should be word-processed and error free. Take advantage of computer-based grammar-checking programs to help edit your narrative and letters.

Recommendation forms should be properly signed and completed. If a school uses a form with a grid, be sure it is completed as requested because this is how many schools obtain a rating score from references. A letter may accompany the form but should not be submitted in lieu of the grid form. Applicants often wonder whether they should allow the recommendation writer confidentiality and waive the right to review the form. Usually, confidentiality is preferable, because the applicant may select who provides the recommendations. Therefore, select recommendation writers whom you feel will support your application. There are cases when specific persons must write recommendations, such as a major professor of a master's program when application is being made to a doctoral program. Under these circumstances, be sure you sit with this person and discuss his or her assessment of your potential for success in a graduate program and what he or she plans to write in the evaluation of you.

Many application packages now require that a candidate's résumé be submitted. The résumé should be current and professional. A professional résumé is a necessary investment you will use often. With modern computer technology, you can create a résumé on disk and then later easily modify it. In most cases, use fonts and paper that would be appropriate for business settings unless you are applying to a graduate program in a field, such as art or advertising, in which visual creativity is important to the program.

Writing samples and portfolios can significantly enhance an applicant's materials. Writing samples may include papers from classes that have been properly evaluated and corrected, published articles, book chapters, training manuals, or other documents that show evidence of the applicant's communication skills. Professionally made videotapes also have been submitted by applicants as indication of media-related competencies. Portfolios that contain newspaper articles, clippings, awards, and community recognitions can be helpful if they are manageable in size, attractively done, and related to the applicant's potential for success in graduate school. For example, portfolios of all the beauty pageants you have won won't do very much to enhance your graduate school application, but a small collection of community service awards you received while you were the reigning queen of whatever may positively influence the admissions committee.

Almost all graduate schools require a standardized test of some type, either the GRE, Graduate Management Aptitude Test (GMAT), Miller's Analogy Test (MAT), GRE subject tests (e.g., biology, physics, psychology, etc.), or another examination, depending on the program. It is important to have your test scores sent directly to the school in a timely manner. The most efficient way is to identify the schools you would like to have your scores sent to when you take the test. It is less costly this way and saves a lot of time and effort. Most graduate schools will not accept your copy of the test results as the official copy, and decisions on admission may be delayed while the school waits for your test scores.

If possible, start the application preparation early so that all of the required documents can be submitted simultaneously. Doing this reduces the chances of materials becoming lost or misfiled. Also, use the same name on all of the documents. Make sure that the documents required from you arrive before recommendations and supporting materials from other sources.

File copies of each piece submitted and keep a record of the date. Establish a telephone log and list all telephone calls and faxes, incoming and outgoing. File all correspondence received for handy reference and in the event that you want to reapply at a subsequent time.

▓ Tips for Increasing Your Chances of Getting in

• Plan to take any required tests, such as the GRE or the GMAT, at least one year before you start the application process. Not all schools require these tests but many do, and you don't want to be eliminated from a good program because of not having taken the test. Typically, these tests are hard and you do need to study for them. Taking the test early gives you the opportunity to take it again if necessary. Don't feel embarrassed about having to take the test more than once. At least half of the people applying to graduate schools have taken it more than once. Many graduate schools take the *best* subtest scores you may have earned over several test administrations to arrive at your official "total" score for admissions purposes. There are a number of schools that officially state that certain standardized tests may be culturally biased and consider that fact when reviewing applicants of color and other cultures. Nevertheless, even here, applicants are considered more favorably if they have attempted the test more than once and showed improvement.

• Application materials must be submitted on or before the required deadlines. If the school offers an early admissions decision deadline, attempt to meet this date if possible. This is usually the pool of applicants that will be drawn on for assistantships, fellowships, and other nonloan funding offers.

• Get to know the admissions director, at least one member on the admissions committee, and a faculty member and alumni who can advocate on your behalf. Contact them regularly, but don't become a pest.

• Visit the school.

• Make sure that your materials look good and are appropriate for the department to which you are applying. Although the personal narrative for each school may contain much of the same information, make sure that it doesn't read as though it were written for another program.

• Get strong recommendation letters. Use professors and professionals with credentials. A letter from the chairperson of the usher board at your church may say wonderful things about you, but it won't help very much in getting you into a competitive graduate school program. Reference letters should speak about a candidate's ability to engage in analytical and abstract thinking and independent study, an applicant's tenacity and thirst for knowledge, the ability for excellent communication in written and oral forms, and other indications of academic excellence. Admissions committees are looking for evidence of scholarship and the ability to do research or practice in a particular field at an advanced level. They want to make sure that if they let you into their graduate program, you can get out by graduating, not by being asked to leave because of poor performance.

• The personal statement or statement of purpose must be organized, concise, well written, and free of grammatical and punctuation errors. This part of the application should be exemplary, because many schools use it as a writing sample. Be informative, but don't use it as a forum to talk about all of the personal problems you have had, which is now why you want to go to graduate school. A small amount of that may be helpful. Too much will be detrimental.

• Apply to more than one school, and if the resources are available, be willing to travel. For example, if you know that your GRE scores are not as high as you would like, apply to some schools that do not require the GRE or rank it as highly in the decision to admit. Apply to some schools that you *know* you can get into. In terms of the long-term success of your career, what you do *after* earning your graduate degree is more important than *where* you got it from.

- If you are still in school while reading this book, one of the best things you can do is make "A" grades in your courses. If you have a choice between focusing on course grades versus student government or community service, go lighter on the campus stuff and heavy on the grades. Graduate programs are usually not looking as closely for the well-rounded student as are undergraduate schools. Graduate schools are looking for scholars, researchers, and practitioners who have specific qualifications.

How Decisions Are Made and What Committees Look For

Different schools have different processes for making decisions, but the two most common forFats involve the admissions committees (made up of faculty, administrators, and/or students who make decisions) and the admissions directors who make decisions with recommendations from faculty. Both groups often have the responsibility for sifting through many applications, reviewing the ones that are qualified, and filling fewer positions than applicants for a graduate program. The committee is typically very crucial in a doctoral program in which as few as from two to four applicants may be accepted for a given year.

A committee or admissions director may use a ranking system or another formalized guide for making decisions. Nevertheless subjectivity still is a part of the process, particularly with large pools of applicants with similar qualifications. For example, if the committee vote is split about a certain applicant and the applicant has made a favorable impression on the chair of the admissions committee, the committee may choose to go with the recommendation of the chair.

The following are some admissions criteria that may be used by departments in making a decision: grade point averages in undergraduate and graduate work, grade point average in the major, GRE or other test scores, recommendations, outstanding academic projects, publications, quality of the personal statement, impressions from face-to-face meetings, quality of the undergraduate or other graduate schools in which the applicant has studied, goals of the applicant, and mission of the school.

What Happens if You Don't Get In Anywhere (or You Are Accepted by Your Least Favorite School)?

Conceivably, an applicant may be accepted by his or her last choice school or not at all. In the first case, evaluate whether it is imperative to go now or to sit out a year and try to improve the factors that weakened the application, such as test scores or less-than-glowing recommendations. The applicant also may consider starting at the less-than-desired school, making excellent grades in a graduate program, and then transferring to another (more desirable) program. Typically, graduate course grades will always pull more weight than undergraduate grades even if the school does not appear to be very prestigious. For many students, this is a better option than sitting out for a year, running the risk of not going at all.

If your application is denied, one strategy is to contact the admissions directors of the prospective schools and make a personal or telephone appointment to discuss your file, not the decision on admissions. Many programs will not give information about why a candidate was denied; therefore, this should not be the focus of your appointment. The goal should be to get recommendations on how you can strengthen your application for graduate school generally; not for the specific school in question. Using these recommendations as a guide, work to correct the deficits, then reapply to some of the same schools and add new schools to the list.

If Accepted

Contact the school about any prerequisite courses or seminars that should be taken before matriculation, and get them completed before school starts. If possible, establish an early relationship with your advisor or a mentor before you arrive. Work out plans for housing, transportation, health insurance, banking, and other basic needs before arriving. Though dormitory living may not be suitable, check to see if the school you are attending offers apartments for graduate students. If so, they are usually convenient and inexpensive.

Once accepted, you should immediately begin to bring closure to the process of finding funding resources which you should have started before applying. Don't make the mistake of waiting to be accepted into graduate school before starting to figure out how it will be paid for.

If relocating to a new city or state, move early enough to get settled and learn your way around campus and the city. Call people you may know, sorority sisters or fraternity brothers, or get referrals from friends who know people where you are going.

FINANCING GRADUATE SCHOOL

▓ A Simple Method to the "Madness"

How to pay for graduate education is probably one of the top three questions every graduate student asks and the one that most lament over. The cost largely depends on whether the school is a private institution or a state university. Graduate education tends to be costly in tuition, books, fees, research projects, and housing. The bottom line is that you will need *some* money, even if you do graduate school on a shoestring.

Students often feel perplexed and helpless when it comes to obtaining money for graduate school. It can be a long, diligent process, but it is not that complex. First, there *is* money out there available for graduate school and lots of it. Millions of dollars go unclaimed each year. The problem is that students make two classic mistakes: they wait too long, and they look in the wrong places.

Your search for graduate school money should begin at least 18 months to 2 years before you plan to attend. Your search for funding actually should begin before you start the process of selecting a school, but most aspiring students do just the opposite—wait until the school selection process has started or even wait until they are accepted before they begin the search for money in earnest. For maximum results, you must start early.

The goal for financing graduate education is not just to get the tuition covered but to get money for books, research, and living expenses. The most important thing is to get enough money so you don't have to incur huge loan debts.

There are several sources of financial support for graduate students, but most African Americans rely solely on the schools or government loans for the money they need. Colleges and universities usually supply money to graduate students through research assistantships, teaching assistantships, nonteaching assistantships, research grants, and other university or departmental grants. These tend to be very competitive, and in the face of affirmative action changes, fewer universities will be working hard to get these monies to African Americans.

Already, we are seeing African American students incur more loan debts. Ten years ago, an African American pursuing graduate education in a large university was almost assured of funding. Now, some estimates say that the average graduate student will incur about $40,000 to $50,000 in debts to finance undergraduate and graduate education. This is an astronomical burden to take with you into the workworld once your education is over.

African American doctoral students are more likely to receive funding from school sources than master's students because of the small size of most doctoral programs and the general feeling that doctoral students should be supported. Because of the money available at different schools around the country, qualified African American doctoral students should not have to accept an offer for admission that comes without funding from the school. Here again, the student may have to shop for more than one school, but the money is available.

So, where does a master's or doctoral candidate look for money outside school assistantships and government loans? The answer is private foundation grants, private scholarships, private research grants, and governmental research grants. Many of these funding sources go year after year without awarding their full supply of money. Usually, it is available by completing a simple application and writing a statement of purpose. The key is that you have to spend the time doing the initial research about funding sources, and you have to start early.

In the reference section of most large university libraries there are several books (probably at least from 15 to 25) with pages and pages and pages describing private and research financial assistance available for graduate students. Addresses and details are provided for how to get applications and access this money. It is a time-consuming but relatively simple process. Once a list is compiled and applications are obtained, usually all that is left is to write the personal statement and have reference letters sent. The body of the personal statement can be said on diskette and modified to fit the particular program. Apply to as many as possible, just crank them out on the word processor.

Here is a small sample of the reference materials available.

The Graduate Scholarship Book (Daniel Cassidy, 1990)

Peterson's Grants for Graduate Students (published yearly, Peterson's Guides, 1996)

Don't Miss Out: The Ambitious Student's Guide to Financial Aid (Leider & Leider, 1989)

Ebony Magazine: Annual Guide to College Scholarships (published yearly)

Questions often arise about applying for financial aid and accepting loans. The college or university financial aid offices at the individual schools are better equipped to answer those specific questions. Nevertheless, beware that most of the educational grant monies are designated for undergraduate students; and financial aid offices almost always want to stick graduate students with loans. Also, these funds are almost always awarded based on the need determined by the Financial Aid Form (FAF) or another standardized need assessment. These tools often work against aspiring graduate students, because they factor in the income an applicant was making prior to matriculation, but don't consider the decreased income when the student will no longer work. The student must have almost an entire year of limited income before graduate school for the tool to accurately assess the need. So, students who were working prior to graduate school rarely benefit from financial aid their first year.

A small piece of advice about loans: incur them only if you have exhausted every other possible funding avenue and this is the only way you can attend graduate school. If you are limited to loans, look for the best school with the lowest price tag, usually a state university where there are no additional fees for out-of-state students. If you start early enough, chances are you may not have to incur loans for your schooling.

AFFIRMATIVE ACTION AND OPPORTUNITY FOR GRADUATE STUDY

Owing to a number of recent court cases and the 1996 California decision to reverse affirmative action, we will see changes in admissions and funding opportunities for African Americans. Predictions are that it will get worse before it gets better. African American students will have to be more focused and set their sights on graduate school early in their undergraduate careers. They will have to make top grades and score well on the standardized tests. These will be the indicators used because of the large number of applicants versus the smaller number of positions available in most graduate schools. Subjective considerations for admission will be inched out of the equation because of the backlash about reverse discrimination.

The reversal of affirmative action is a dangerous posture in many aspects for African Americans. It will affect the opportunities for training of scholars, researchers, and professionals who need the graduate credentials. Colleges and universities that are really committed to serving people of color will still find a way to make sure African Americans are admitted and funded. We'll see which schools believe in justice and which ones spout empty rhetoric. Nevertheless, current African American scholars and researchers cannot leave it up to external sources to make sure we have a continuing legacy of credentialed professionals. They must mentor, support, and guide younger African American students who are now making choices that must sustain them in the future.

ACCEPT NO LIMITATIONS

Despite affirmative action and its backlash, the tediousness of selecting the right school, and the complexity of locating money for graduate education, African Americans must move forward in receiving advanced academic credentials. The key to success in this area is no mystery. It is a scientific process that brings accurate results when you properly execute it. Despite the changing social and political environment with its potential to alter the country's landscape and negatively affect African Americans, we must accept no limitations.

3

DEVELOPING A MASTER PLAN

THE IMPORTANCE OF A MASTER PLAN

Once you've picked a school, are settled, and are ready to begin, you may wonder why you need a master plan. And what is this master plan anyway? Shouldn't meeting with your advisor and mapping out your course schedule be enough? If only graduate school were as simple as that.

The master plan is the document that will guide you through the entire graduate school process. It is a road map. It not only sketches the courses you plan to take and the sequence in which you plan to take them, it pinpoints when you think you will serve an internship, take comprehensive exams, or gather the data for your thesis or dissertation. The master plan is important because it forces you to plan not only the academic portions of the process but also living arrangements, funding, and other details necessary for your survival.

Why Do You Need a Master Plan?

- Graduate school is one activity in a chain of events that will make up your life. Having a plan for graduate school will help you maximize the events to follow.

- You will finish faster, provided you stick to the plan.
- It will make the process easier by organizing your responsibilities and requirements and identifying the resources that you need.
- A master plan will help you stay focused, "the eyes on the prize" concept.
- You have an idea of who you need to meet and make connections with, because you understand how the graduate school experience will be helpful in meeting your life goals.
- A master plan helps with time management, allowing the opportunity to have time for leisure and relaxation.
- A master plan will provide documentation of all work and milestones you accomplished.
- A master plan will safeguard your sanity and the sanity of those who love and support you.

A MASTER PLAN FORMAT

There are several formats for a master plan, but typically one would include a monthly and weekly calendar, a list of all the significant events listed one year at a time, goals to be accomplished, and a smaller plan within the larger one generally thought of as an action plan. Action plans list specific tasks to be completed as means to accomplishing overall goals. Action plans should be organized and accessible. Keep them in a tool, such as a daily organizer or a binder. Regular appointment books typically are not helpful because they do not afford the space for the narrative kind of writing you need to do. Update your master and action plans at least monthly.

SETTING GOALS AND ESTABLISHING PRIORITIES: KEY PARTS OF THE PLAN

Goal setting for the graduate school process should include a 5-to-10-year span. Although the primary goal may be to get the degree, if that's all you do, you will not have maximized your experience. You should begin the process by having an idea about the nature of the profession you will engage in after graduate school. After all, you selected your particular field of study and it was selected for some good reason.

With an idea in mind about the field and profession of interest, begin visualizing what you see yourself doing and who you will be 5 years after receiving the degree. On a sheet of paper, list those things you see. They become your long-range or middle-range goals, depending on the type of person you are. Then, begin asking yourself what it will take to make those dreams come true. List them. They become your long or middle-range activities.

Once you have those, assess which of the activities are absolutely vital to your long-range goals. List those activities that can be accomplished in graduate school. Look for activities that can be performed while also fulfilling the requirements of school. Fit those activities into the weekly and monthly schedule and the yearly calendar. For those activities that will require additional effort, look to see if you can complete them during breaks or while studying for your comprehensive exams.

Here is an example of how one student set goals.

Both my parents were college professors and I knew that I wanted to be a college professor as well. I also knew that I wanted to be a specialist and consultant in the area of autistic children. I had a master's degree in early childhood and was ready to get on with my dreams.

Long-range goals: *College professor and outside consultant generating additional dollars through speaking engagements and program development.*

Qualifications needed: *PhD in developmental psychology, certificate courses in developmental disabilities in children, a track record of conference presentations and publications, experience on a development project.*

Activities necessary: *Get doctorate, enroll in certificate courses in other departments, get a mentor in my area of interest, do dissertation on autism, present at a minimum of three conferences while in the doctoral program, get two publications while in school, do voluntary internship in agency doing program development for autistic children.*

Student's action plan:

What	When
1. Begin doctoral program	Fall Semester 1996
2. Select mentor	Winter 1997
3. Develop complete program of study	Winter 1997
4. Begin electives outside department	Summer 1997
5. Submit 1st paper for publication	Fall 1997
6. Finalize dissertation topic	Fall 1997
7. Make 1st conference presentation	Winter 1998
8. Finish electives outside department	Summer 1998
9. Submit 2nd paper for publication	Fall 1998
10. Start internship	Fall 1998
11. Finish internship	Winter 1999
12. Complete course work & take comprehensive examinations	Spring 1999
13. Start dissertation	Summer 1999
14. Make 2nd conference presentation	Winter 2000
15. Graduate	Spring 2000

Note: Action plans are not written in stone and should be revised as necessary. Also, good program management requires a more detailed daily, weekly, and monthly schedule.

CREATING A PROGRAM OF STUDY THAT FITS YOUR PLAN

Standard course offerings in your department may not provide the depth for the kind of skills and expertise you want to develop. Don't be afraid to look outside your department, as permitted, to build a program of study that fits your master plan. This may be essentially easy once you have completed the required core courses for your degree. Many students opt to take courses like these during the summer semesters.

Another possibility is to learn from prominent professors in your interest area through independent study courses. Internships and fellowships are often available in certain fields as well. Students receive funding while engaging in specialized research or learning opportunities.

Furthermore, many universities offer transient student programs, in which students can enroll at another university and take a limited number of courses that can be transferred in without penalty. This flexibility provides not only the chance to gain relevant course information but also the opportunity to hear new perspectives, meet other colleagues, and network.

WORKING THE MASTER PLAN

Plans are only good if one takes the time to execute them. Things to do include the following:

Meet with your faculty advisor and mentor regularly.

Set up a schedule that includes time for class work, studying, and a social life.

Get organized and stay that way; order your living space, work space, briefcase, car, and so forth.

Buy yourself a daily organizer or other time management type appointment book or organizer and use it.

Post your year-at-a-glance action plan in a visible location so that you see it every day.

Devise a detailed daily, weekly, and monthly schedule.

Create a work and study environment suitable for peak performance.

Establish a filing system and keep all important documents. (Very important.)

Make and use a daily or weekly "to do" list system.

Exercise as much self-discipline as you can.

Do what the plan says, but be open to helpful changes.

If you fall off the plan, figure out a way to cover lost ground and get moving again.

STARTING OFF ON THE RIGHT FOOT

If you want to maximize your chances for successfully completing your course work, taking exams, and writing your thesis or dissertation, you must have a plan. The plan should be comprehensive, achievable, and smart enough to help you stay in the game without unnecessary struggle.

4

Staying In The Game

With Robert Brandau

TO THINE OWN SELF BE TRUE

This chapter is about the human supports necessary for staying in the game. One essential support is the self-validation that one offers oneself every day that by seeking graduate education he or she is doing something valuable, not just for oneself but for the greater good of society. This self-validation more often comes with ease when people feel good about the choices *they* make for themselves. Choices that support the innermost desires of their hearts. Choices that are not driven by fear but choices driven by the passion of something hoped for.

Though maneuvering through graduate school is exciting, challenging, and exhilarating. It also can be a tricky time when one can lose his or her way and the important image of self. Graduate students have to balance maintaining their individuality and being molded by peers, mentors, major professors, committees, and other representatives of their prospective fields.

Graduate school is an important developmental phase. Get an image in your mind of who you are now and who you hope to be. Decide which things are negotiable and which are not. Be clear about the price that you are willing to pay for anything, because remember, nothing in life is free. Develop your own dream, never letting fear stand in your way. Be committed to your passion without ceasing. To thine own self be true.

A fun way of getting an image in your mind of who you are and hope to be is to create a treasure map. Treasure maps can serve as visual reminders of the transformational goals and desires that you have established for yourself. It puts your thoughts into pictures which gives you something real to focus on and can be changed often. You may add things or take them away, based on the fine-tuning of your goals. Put it on your mirror or on your bulletin board. Make a copy of it and carry it in your portfolio for constant reinforcement. Share it with your mentor as a developmental starting point. Most of all, use it or any other similar tool to help you stay focused on *your* dreams.

MENTORSHIP: FOLLOWING THE PATH

One of the most common complaints heard from African American students is that they do not know what to do to ensure success once they get to graduate school. They have some general idea about grades being important and a vague notion of the kinds of assignments, but they feel lost about how to get information about specific details. After giving it some thought, I can understand what they mean.

For example, I have been studying the use of herbal remedies and natural medicine for the last 5 years. And though I've read many books and magazines, I often find myself in the health food store asking, "Why don't they put explicit directions on these things?" It would be extremely simple if the bottle said, "For headaches, take two cups of this with orange juice twice per day at 8:00 A.M. and 8:00 P.M. Take it for 10 days. The headaches should subside in 7 days, but continue taking the dosage for 10 days." Unfortunately, the remedies very rarely read this way. Usually, it's more like this: "May be used for headaches, may be taken under the tongue, or in liquids, or may be taken as a tea." Too many possibilities—I wanted someone to say, "If you want these results, then do this and this and this."

Not enough specifics are often the same scenario for many graduate students. And, it's normal to be unsure about how to do something, particularly if you have never done it. We spend a great deal of time telling students how different graduate school is from undergraduate studies, but we don't spend enough time explaining how it is different or what to do about it.

As I was having this discussion with a colleague of mine, she also made a good point. She reminded me that many African American graduate students are first-generation graduate scholars in their families and some of them are first-generation college scholars in their families. We were the first to go. Though our parents and siblings may have been extremely proud of us, they could not offer the technical advice and field of study wisdom on how to maneuver through graduate school. The point is an important one and it makes a lot of sense. I didn't have anyone in my family to depend on for that information, because so far as I know, I am the first with a doctoral degree on either side of my family, and no one in my family had a master's degree before I had mine. My mother went on to get her master's degree in business education, but this was several years after I already had received my master's.

So, how do African American students get this vital information? One solution is through mentoring programs, either formal programs or informal mentor relationships. The term *mentor* first came from Greek mythology. Mentor was the loyal friend and advisor of Odysseus, a great soldier who won many battles. Since then, mentor has come to mean teacher, advisor, or coach, one who guides and points the way. Throughout the course of history, we can identify several notable mentor relationships. And though there are few empirical studies of their effectiveness, there are enough personal accounts out there that lead us to believe that mentor relationships may significantly affect the success of individuals who experience them.

Consider the example of resilient children. Take the case of the "A family" living intergenerationally in a violent, crime-ridden, drug-infested housing project. The parents in the "A family" are extremely dysfunctional and do not value education. Children are equally dysfunctional, exhibiting qualities that generally indicate to most folks that "they won't amount to anything." But, one child gets out—excels in school against the odds with no support from family, eventually goes on to medical school, and becomes a brilliant surgeon. What happened? People who have studied the phenomenon say two factors are most often present: a burning internal desire for a better life that cannot be extinguished and a relationship with someone who exhibits the qualities of success that the child values.

African American graduate students need that relationship. A good graduate school mentor seeks to develop qualities of success in students while attempting to nourish and fan the flames of that burning internal desire. Mentors seek to point the way by combining facts and experiential learning to give students the truth about what to expect in graduate school and the world outside. Mentor relationships often continue far beyond graduate school and may last a lifetime.

Characteristics of a Good Mentor Relationship

The mentor has the desire to serve as teacher, coach, loyal advisor, and guide. The student has the desire to learn from the teacher.

There is mutual respect and admiration and both see potential and qualities of success in each other.

The mentor and the student are committed to the relationship and the best interest of each other.

The mentor is willing to continue in his or her own development to help the student maneuver in a changing world.

There is an open line of communication in which the mentor is willing to speak the truth and the student is willing to hear it and sometimes vice versa. It is a safe place to laugh, cry, challenge, and learn.

The mentor relationship is a valuable receptacle for storing nourishment, information, and resources.

Advice on Finding a Mentor

1. Make the decision that you need one.
2. Spend time in self-evaluation, deciding what your interests are and what qualities you think are important for success.
3. Visualize the kind of relationship that you would like to have with your mentor. What do you want it to feel like? Determine the benefits you hope to receive from the mentor relationship.
4. Begin meeting with people who may be potential mentors. Visit them in their offices. Ask questions. Invite them to lunch. Your intent is to discover whether you can get along.
5. Look for a person who shares your interests and the success qualities you identified, but if you are not able to find one person, don't be afraid to have two mentors.

Mentorship Activities

- Assisting in creating a development plan
- Orientating to the graduate school
- Providing the "inside scoop" on the school

- Acquainting the student with the field, profession, or both
- Helping to develop research topics
- Providing writing assistance
- Reading papers, listening to presentations, and giving feedback
- Offering opportunities for publishing and presenting papers
- Helping to develop problem-solving skills
- Teaching political savvy
- Listening
- Assessing situations and identifying outcomes, rewards, and consequences, academic and personal
- Performing other duties as necessary

■ Ancillary Duties

- Friend
- Fashion consultant
- Computer guru
- Pseudoparent
- Psychic
- Love life advisor
- Cheerleader

THE PERILS OF GOING IT ALONE: YOU NEED STUDENT SUPPORT

Graduate school can sometimes feel like a very lonely place, and isolation can be common if students don't take the proper precautions. Students who are isolated often become depressed, frustrated, and report a high level of stress. Once this happens, the risk of dropping out becomes much greater.

Graduate school is different from undergraduate education in that it is normal for many graduate students to be going to school, working, balancing families, and tending to lives that were already in full swing before they started school. For African American students, it may be even more isolating because many of them attend predominantly white institutions, where they may be one of only a few black students in their programs. Incoming doctoral classes are usually very small, most ranging from 6 to 15 students. It would be almost phenomenal to find several blacks in an incoming doctoral class at a predominantly white university.

Feelings of isolation for graduate students may occur on any campus despite its racial composition, because there are few planned activities outside class for graduate students, and they almost all scream that even if there were more, what grad student would really have time to attend them anyway? Ninety percent of them would if they learned to manage their time better and understood the benefits of solidarity.

Master's-level graduate students may feel trapped in the middle of a school's student body. They are expected to have moved beyond the undergraduate mindset with its activities, but they are not really accepted at the level of doctoral students. Further, many master's students attend part-time and may pop in for classes and then go about the business of attending to their lives, making themselves unavailable to others and resources unavailable to them. Also, in master's and doctoral programs, once the course work is finished, students progress through the program at different times, based on whether they need to take 6 months to study for their comprehensive exams, and so forth. So, once the course work is over, there is really no sense of togetherness. This is a very difficult time to feel alone.

Graduate students need support from their peers. Student support helps to decrease feelings of isolation. No matter how good a mentor, professors, major professor, or committee they may have, students need someone on their level to bounce ideas off of, do reality testing on, commiserate with, learn from, and just hang out.

A wise graduate student will have more than one support group. You need at least one from your particular program to help decode information, serve as a study partner, be a frame of reference, and begin establishing a network of colleagues that will support you not only in graduate school but also once you move into your professional career.

One of the most exciting ideas about the benefits of supports is the concept of mastermind groups that I first read about in Napoleon Hill's book *Laws of Success* (which, by the way, I highly recommend you read). In summary, a group of aspiring young men came together often for many years to support each other, discuss ideas, and raise their thinking level. They scheduled retreats and mastermind sessions away from families, friends, and business associates. They were very committed to each other and to using their collective minds for solving problems, creating wealth, and experiencing a better way of living. It's also important to know that they all saw the vision of success for themselves *and* for each other. These now famous men were Andrew Carnegie, John Paul Getty, Charles Schwab, and the list goes on and on.

Establish a supportive relationship with graduate students outside your department. This allows you to know other people, and when your classmates disappear you still have other friends. Relationships such as these also provide additional opportunities not only to enhance the graduate school experience but to learn the skills needed for networking and coalition building in the employment arena.

Join graduate student organizations. Become a part of political action groups. If time permits, do volunteer work in the community. This is an excellent way to build supports. Become active in or join fraternities or sororities if they appeal to you. The bottom line is: Don't go it alone.

There is something to be said about solidarity—being united with people of like mind. It is the concept that Hill (1900) talked about. The civil rights movement progressed because of it. Political action committees in this country win important battles because of it. Social change occurs through it. African American graduate students should learn to use it.

1-800-HELLO: KEEPING A LIFELINE
TO FRIENDS AND FAMILY

Some very simple advice needed for helping to survive graduate school: Stay in touch. You would be surprised to see how important mail and communication from people outside the graduate school setting become. A letter from home or a phone call from an old friend can be paramount. Because once you get into graduate school, people try to cut you off. They think you don't need them anymore, graduate school means "adult school." If you are not careful, the routine check-ins (and checks!) stop coming, they stop calling every week to keep you posted on family events, and they rarely send airplane tickets for you to come home for all the important holidays. They see you as all grown up now that you are in graduate school.

I remember when I went to grad school, my mother went with me to help set up my apartment. This was a happy time for me—a grad student, my first apartment, had my own car, I was on top of the world until my mother delivered the crashing blow. We were sitting around the new "crib" (it was a "crib" in those days) just relaxing, when my mother informed me "You still have plenty of time before school starts to find a little job."

Little job! Was she kidding? Obviously not, when I saw the amount of the check she gave me for spending money. On a snack allowance similar to that of someone in a nursing home, that check would have lasted me about 3 weeks. I needed a lot more spending money than that.

I did have some money stashed, having worked as a camp counselor over the summer, but I didn't want to chance it in the event that my mother wasn't bluffing. So I got a job in the toy department of a big discount store. That was the beginning of the end of regular checks from the folks. And not only did the cash dry up but because I became busier and didn't have the time to write, people didn't write to me either. So, not only was I on "cash hold" but "news-and-gossip hold" as well.

Nevertheless, don't worry; this does not have to be your fate. Here is a scientific, foolproof plan guaranteed to keep the cash and news flowing. Step 1: At the beginning of the school year, go to the bookstore and buy envelopes with your school insignia on them. Buy enough so you can make a set of 12 for each grandparent or aging relative with money. This works particularly well with grandmothers. Step 2: Address them to you and deliver as many sets in person as you can. Explain how much you love school and them, but you'll be too busy to visit often. Casually explain that you know how much they like to send you a "little spending change," so you already addressed the envelopes. They can send it off when they mail their bills. Works like a charm. Step 3: Get a card for each holiday and have a box of note cards on hand. Send cards on the holidays, and on the off months send "thinking-of-you" cards. Each month when *you* mail your bills, send thank-you notes. Oh, and by the way, be sure to call and say you got the money and you love them. Call collect; they look forward to saying they will accept the charges. I remember my grandmother and her friends talking about it with great pride.

Using the same concept, buy postcards and address them to family and friends. Send them out whenever you accomplish a milestone, any milestone, no matter how small it may seem to you. It's cheaper than calling and keeps people updated and aware of your progress without having to write long, drawn out letters unless you want to and time permits. Then, folks hearing from you often feel the need to keep you updated, so they write and give you news about what you are missing. Those who don't write will call. Also, ask people to give you prepaid calling cards as part of holiday gifts. They are convenient, easy to buy, and people love knowing that you will be calling them regularly.

Don't take for granted how important it is to stay connected during the graduate school process with those who support and care about you. I was always happy to share the good news with family and friends. And when things got tough, I needed to hear my mother's voice. She had a special way of reminding me that everything would be all right. Family and friends reinforced for me that the time and energy were worth it and that I was doing a great thing. Many days, this is what kept me in the game.

KEEPING YOUR FINANCES IN CHECK
SO YOU CAN STAY IN THE GAME

Financial worries can impede or even cause an end to your pursuit of educational goals. Before beginning your education, it is wise to take stock of your financial situation. If necessary, take steps to rectify any outstanding debts and financial demands. Being free of money worries will allow you to focus your energy and time toward your course work.

Most people are not able to work a full-time job while going to graduate school. The schooling itself might be limiting because of the amount of time required to study or attend class. There are other considerations, such as family, community involvement, and so forth. All these things have a direct bearing on your earning potential. The basic questions that must be asked center on your practical pursuit of an advanced degree and your current living standard. It might be necessary to temporarily revamp your way of life to accommodate your educational goals. Weigh carefully the time and money commitments involved in your schooling efforts. Both have a serious impact on each other. Are you prepared to take a cut in salary to go back to school? This is a distinct possibility.

Perhaps you are among the majority of Americans who carry some credit card debt or the many whose debt load consumes more of their disposable income than is comfortable. The misuse of credit cards or a pileup of installment payments, such as car loans, may be the cause of your difficulties. It is also possible that you simply may have been hit by unexpectedly high legal fees, medical bills, or home repairs. Whatever the cause, what can you do to get out of the financial hole?

Get the things under control that got you into debt in the first place. Pay off any new charges each month. Limit the use of cards or better yet, quit using them entirely. Resolve not to buy anything on the installment plan. The best policy is to pay cash. There is actually very little one needs that cannot wait until there is cash on hand to buy it. Think twice before buying that new suit or new chair. Yes, it might look good, or be impressive to your friends and family, but the monthly bills are constant reminders of your unnecessary purchases.

Create a workable budget, and be determined to stick to it. Get a handle on your spending habits. Once you can do this, you can probably target areas to cut expenses. Is the expensive car more important to you than earning a degree. Despite the advertising ploys, remember, transportation that gets you from point "A" to "B" is all you really need. Sell that expensive car or quit buying a new one every 2 years. A well-maintained car is cheaper than making a high car payment month after month. Also, consider that a bigger, more expensive car demands a higher insurance premium. Brown-bag your lunch, eat at home more often. Consider learning more about inexpensive but nutritious ways to prepare food. This is a subtle but easy way to lower personal expenditures. Buy fewer clothes or ones that are less expensive. Buy clothes that are multiseasonal or clothes that are more traditional and stay in style longer. Remember, your main ambition should be to clothe your mind with an education. People will remember what you contribute intellectually much longer than what you wore to the last Christmas party.

Bring expenditures below income so you can put extra money toward your debts. Learn to say no to friends who place unfair demands on your financial resources. If necessary, get a second job or work extra hours to generate more income. You might have to postpone some course work in favor of getting your financial house in order. Although it sounds romantic, the "starving student" complex should be left to writers of novels. If you do not have money, you will end giving up your educational dreams out of necessity.

Start lowering your debts. Pay off an initial debt as quickly as possible, perhaps using a tax refund, a bonus check, or extra monthly cash flow generated by cutting expenses. Continue making all other monthly payments as you were doing before. Once the initial debt is paid, add that payment to the one on the next debt until it is also paid. You can fold down debts in different sequences. Paying off the debt with the highest interest rate first saves the most money in the long run. It may be psychologically easier, though, to start with the one with the smallest balance or the fewest payments. That way, progress can be seen more quickly.

If you cannot make the required payments, you may be able to negotiate lower, prorated installments. As an example, after appropriate belt-tightening, you might be able to afford $300 a month toward total debts of $6,000. That means you can make prorated payments of 5% for each creditor. If you owe a particular creditor $3,000, your prorated payment would be $150 a month. Most creditors are agreeable to prorating payments. Prorating does not always work on secured loans, such as for a car. The creditor may decide to repossess the property. Be mindful how you approach this subject with your creditors.

Consolidate your debts. If you have several credit cards, it might be possible to pay them off by moving the balance to a single card. Check the interest rates and the credit limit and then consolidate if possible. Destroy the old cards and make sure you close the old accounts. This will prevent you from being tempted to use them again and accumulate additional debt. If you own your home, you can consolidate debts with an equity loan. This type of loan typically carries a lower interest rate and is usually tax deductible. You may be able to borrow at reasonable rates from your retirement plan or the cash value of your life insurance. Before doing this, be sure to review the costs and other potential financial ramifications of these choices thoroughly. Pay attention to interest rates. Be careful that you do not consolidate several low interest rate debts at a higher single rate. The consolidated payment should be smaller than the total of all payments over the same period. Some types of debts are interest free, such as some physician or lawyer fees. It would not make sense to consolidate them to an interest-bearing loan.

Although not recommended, there might be a possibility of a "family" loan. Depending on your relationship and the reasons for requesting the money, family members might be willing to help by lending you money or by helping you secure a loan from a lending institution. Be wary of this route. By involving others in your goals, you obligate yourself not only financially but also emotionally. Banks and credit unions lend money as a matter of business. Family members usually do so because of trust, love, or other emotional reasons. Each way has its associated costs and risks.

Having your financial house in order allows you to concentrate more fully on the task at hand. Earning an education takes dedication, discipline, and, it cannot be forgotten, money. Although stipends, scholarships, and other sources of money may be available to assist, you still must cover such basics as housing, food, and transportation. Create a financial plan and incorporate it as part of your educational pursuit.

TAKING CARE OF YOUR BODY
KEEPS YOU IN THE GAME

Many African Americans are beginning to understand the importance of proper diet, nutrition, and exercise. Culturally, most of us have eaten foods and engaged in lifestyles that were not conducive to optimum health. High blood pressure, heart disease, cancer, alcoholism, and substance abuse have been major killers in our community. Further, stress is crippling and exacerbates other medical conditions.

Graduate school is a large-scale stressor for most people. There are numerous deadlines, projects, and obligations to meet. Also, there is often a great deal of anxiety about whether a paper was good enough or whether the grade was above the required "B" average that most graduate programs follow.

To survive graduate school, not only does your mind have to be sharp but your body also has to be ready for the test. Do some research about diet and nutrition that promote optimum health in African Americans. Interestingly enough, we are now being told that the "four food groups" we were taught as children are all wrong. Learn to eat better and add the supplements or vitamins that your body may need.

Develop an exercise program you can follow daily. Most schools have several facilities and programs that students can access. Get involved in intramural sports or start a sports team in your department. Exercise not only increases your body's stamina but is also a great stress buster. This is important in graduate school.

BE A GOOD CITIZEN

An important way to stay in the game is to know that you are involved in the processes of ensuring social equity and justice and making a contribution to others while you are in graduate school. The satisfaction of knowing that you are giving something while you are obtaining your graduate education lifts your self-esteem and reinforces your value to society.

There are several activities that graduate students may become involved in that are extremely vital to communities and campus environments. Graduate students are useful and knowledgeable volunteers for many community programs ranging from Big Brothers or Big Sisters to literacy action councils. They can serve as educators, community organizers, and labor for projects that really make a difference, such as NAACP-sponsored Voter Registration Drives and Habitat for Humanity. After all, graduate school is an environment that can serve as a "good dry run" for the real world beyond school. The discipline and commitment established here can set the stage for success after graduation.

On campus, graduate students can serve as mentors to individual undergrads or to groups of undergrads, such as fraternities and sororities. For example, in light of hazing incidents around the country, graduate students can interject maturity and objectivity in situations involving groups of younger students who may be considering bad decisions. By working in cooperatives and with faculty in various departments, graduate students can assist in bringing quality speakers, educational experiences, and cultural events to campuses. Graduate students also have the responsibility to champion the rights and changes on behalf of undergraduates not as far along the path.

In short, becoming involved in the community and campus is very important. The opportunity provides a vital means for exchanging time and energy for elevated self-worth and sense of value to the world. Involvement such as this also leads to meeting several people helpful in gathering information, networking, and advancing one's educational or professional career. Often persons who are met in these situations become employers or valuable references in the future. More important, they often become lifelong friends that offer a special bond and connection reminding us of the significance of the graduate school experience.

MAKING UP YOUR MIND TO STAY IN THE GAME SETS YOU UP FOR A WIN

Graduate school survivors have to make a conscious effort to do what it takes to get through the process. It requires planning, information, commitment, and action. Do some reflective thinking about the specifics you need to stay in the game. Get a mentor, stay connected to family and friends, keep your financial house in order, take care of your body, and give back to the community.

5

KNOW WHEN TO
LEAVE THE PARTY

LOVING YOURSELF . . . REGARDLESS

Graduate school has the potential to beat up on us. Nevertheless, we are the ones who determine whether we let it. Sure, there are rigorous requirements, exams, papers, a thesis, a dissertation, deadlines, and stress, but we can choose to see the experience another way. We can choose to see it as a game to be played, enjoyed, and won. And we can choose to see ourselves as winners.

Most successful athletes describe their formula for winning as a combination of skill, being in the right place at the right time, luck, and confidence. They see skill as the mastery of the fundamentals of the game. Being in the right place at the right time is anticipating the moves of others, or the ball, or the depth of the course. Luck comes when one tries to do the right thing in life, and athletes see confidence as loving themselves enough to believe that they are the best. Further, not only do they love themselves; they believe that the fans love them too.

The athlete's formula for success can be easily applied to graduate school. It becomes particularly easy to execute when one begins with loving oneself enough to believe that he or she is the best. Some have already learned that lesson. This puts them a few steps ahead on the graduate school survival course. For others, loving themselves is a tough feat. Many of us have scars from the past that make this a difficult thing to do. Maybe we grew up in abusive households or were abandoned or experienced the trauma of death at an early age. Maybe we grew up in poverty having to struggle, and now we believe that struggle is the only way. Others of us may not have been taught that we are special, so we haven't had the practice of loving ourselves. Still others of us who thought we were pretty good at loving ourselves didn't get the real test until we got to the dissertation.

The important thing here is to know that you can be the best and that life is not meant to be a struggle. It is meant to be cherished, enjoyed, and savored. And graduate school, with all of its challenges, does not have to be an event to be struggled through either. The key is not to dwell on the past but to focus on loving ourselves in the here and now. If you want to make graduate school and the rest of your life the exhilarating experience that I've talked about, you've got to put the time in working on the love factor.

Susan Taylor wrote in *In the Spirit* (1993),

> Self-love. It is the starting point for giving love to others. It opens the door to abundant living. Without it we limp through life, becoming part of the walking wounded, the living dead. Self-love. Our cornerstone. We can't grow or glow without it. It determines how solid and fulfilling our lives are. It's the foundation on which we build all the rest. (p. 35)

Self-love is the thing that makes you feel worthy to be at graduate school and deserving of the graduate assistantship, fellowship, and other financial awards. Worthy not just because of the color of your skin but because you are gifted, talented, and have a contribution to make to society. Self-love is what gives you the confidence to network and build relationships with people who can mentor and guide you. Self-love gives you the stamina to keep going on the days when you really want to give up. Self-love gives you the ability to walk away from your committee without breaking, knowing that you'll be back when they reject your draft another time. Self-love gives you the audacity to "strut your stuff" at the dissertation defense. Self-love gives you the grace and gratitude to be able to say thanks to all of the people who helped get you through.

▓ Prescriptions for Learning to Love Yourself

• Begin each day by hugging yourself, calling your name aloud any number of times that feels comfortable to you, and saying "I love you" to yourself. Repeat this exercise mentally during the day whenever you have a chance. Stop waiting for others to say they love you to validate your worth. It's great when others tell you they love you, but you have to experience self-love first, or you won't even believe it when they say it. Ever been in relationships with others, being honest, loving, and true, and no matter how many times you tell them you love them, they still don't believe it? They don't believe it because they don't love themselves enough to actually believe deep down that they are worthy of love and that someone can honor and cherish them; someone unlike all of the other people that hurt them before. Not only does this hold true for romantic relationships but in friendships and collegial relationships as well. I can think of more than one collegial relationship in which people questioned the motives of anyone who genuinely cared for them and tried to help and put up hurdles so high that Edwin Moses and Gail Devers together couldn't get over them.

• It is also particularly helpful to use the mirror when working on self-love. Get in front of the mirror for 5 minutes in the morning and 5 minutes at night, look yourself straight in the eye and tell yourself that you love you. It may seem uncomfortable at first, but do it anyway.

• Make a list of all the things that you would do to show someone special that you love him or her. Then, do as many of them as you can for yourself routinely. Take yourself on a trip or out for a candlelight dinner. Buy yourself flowers. Take relaxing baths with candlelight, soft music, and hot oils. Show yourself that you cherish and love the person that you are.

• Accentuate your strengths and make a plan to enhance those things that you can change. Learn to accept and see positively the things that you can't.

• Release the past and move on by forgiving yourself, people, places, and events. Hate and resentment use a great deal of energy that you could be using for loving.

• Honor yourself by learning to say "no." You will feel a dramatic rise in your self-esteem when you stop doing things that you do not want to do.

• Find your true place in life and live out your purpose.

- Try to make only promises that you can keep. One of the surest ways to demolish your self-worth is to feel that you always let everyone down.
- Have balance in your life. Work smart and play hard.
- Laugh, but don't be afraid to cry. Realize that every opportunity, either good, bad, or indifferent, is the chance to learn a lesson. Don't judge, just learn.
- Make a commitment to give love to others but not before you have given love to yourself.

TAPPING YOUR INNER POWER

Spirituality is different from religion, because it does not espouse a specific doctrine or dogma. Where the two are the same is in the belief that something greater than the human self of any of us gives us the power to succeed. A discussion about either religion or spirituality is a complicated issue in a book about graduate school. And in fact, I couldn't find one that addressed it. Nevertheless, even in the complexity of it, I will say this, because it is important to the African American heritage and culture.

> Whatever your belief about religion or spirituality, find something that you can hold on to, and use it every day. Faith is an extremely important tool to use in graduate school and you must know how to put it into practice. You have to believe in a philosophy that teaches you how to know peace and a philosophy that says without a doubt that you have the power to master any circumstance. The abundance of the universe is yours, including graduate school, waiting for you to rise up and claim it. You have a strength inside that will help you excel in any situation and you can access that power.

In years past, there were few African American authors out there writing directly and specifically about the need and techniques for tapping your inner power. Today, there are several fine authors writing on the subject. Check out a few of my favorites.

In the Spirit (Susan L. Taylor, 1993)
Lessons in Living (Susan L. Taylor, 1995)
Value in the Valley (Iyanla VanZant, 1995)

Transform Your Life (Barbara L. King, 1995)
Black Pearls Journal (Eric V. Copage, 1995)

EVERYTHING IN ITS PROPER PLACE, INCLUDING YOUR SOCIAL LIFE

Rev. Dr. Barbara L. King (1995), an internationally known leader, minister, and orator, always claims that you have got to know when to leave the party. In other words, you have got to know when enough is enough and you need to go home. She told a hilariously funny story about everything she had to do one night trying to get home from a party before sunup while she was a graduate student at Atlanta University (now Clark/Atlanta University). The point of her story, and an important one, was that it's all right to have a good time, but don't indulge in such excess that you forget your responsibilities and obligations in the process.

You need a social life in graduate school. You need an outlet to release stress and pressure and connect with other people. Graduate school should not be drudgery but an exhilarating experience. All work and no play does make Jane a dull girl, no doubt about that. Nevertheless, very few Janes and probably not too many Jacks have survived graduate school opening and closing down every party on campus.

I also want to equate the idea of knowing when to leave the party with learning to say "no." Graduate students often feel that they have to say "yes" to many things that they really don't want to do. You can say no to professors who want you to run personal errands as part of graduate assistantship duties. You can say no to classmates who don't pull their fair share of the load. You can say no to toxic friends and lovers. These are all examples of knowing when to leave the party by saying no.

ALCOHOL, DRUGS, AND GRADUATE SCHOOL

No long, drawn out lecture here. Nancy Reagan already told you what to do: "Just say No to drugs." Students report that marijuana is still being used on college campuses, but it is becoming rather dated in many African American circles. Many upwardly mobile African Americans don't smoke it, and they don't associate with people who do. As for graduate students, it's still illegal and there are no empirical studies that show marijuana as a causal factor in successfully completing master's and doctoral programs.

Alcohol, however, is a different story. Because it is a legal "drug" of choice, it is often found at graduate school functions though it also does not have the honor of being able to promote successful scholars. Again, everything in moderation. Remember that alcohol is a depressant rather than a stimulant, so plan accordingly when you are going to drink and work at the same time. Also, it goes without saying, don't drink and drive.

GRADUATE SCHOOL AND YOUR LOVE LIFE

From recent interviews I conducted with 25 male and 25 female African Americans who finished graduate school in the last year, I was asked by students to pass on the following information. First, I was told to cut right to the chase in this section; no time to waste and no mistakes to be made (I took that to mean this is an important issue). Heartaches and graduate school generally do not mix, especially at the thesis or dissertation stage of the process.

According to the students who were interviewed and several others I have spoken to during the last few years, the most pressing love life worry of students in graduate school is "keeping whom they have"; this goes for people who are married and also those in committed relationships, heterosexual or gay. The stress goes even double for people who are just dating and haven't made a firm pledge to each other or the relationship. They really have a hard time hanging in there with someone trying to build a relationship and maneuver the rigors of graduate school.

Graduate school requires a lot of time and energy. It requires sacrifice, focus, and planned attention to the activities of the degree. These are some of the same requirements as relationships. It's a massive juggling act to do well in school and nurture a relationship at the same time. The fact that many students may go away to graduate school and are in long-distance relationships can be even more of a strain.

Relationships are important. They add special things to life. It's nice to have someone to share accomplishments with, or someone who will comfort you when you cry, or someone to have fun and laugh with. Intimate relationships can provide the support and encouragement helpful to survive graduate school. Some studies indicate that in doctoral programs, married students or students in supportive, loving, encouraging relationships are less likely than single students to drop out. But, graduate school can create the climate for destructive turmoil in relationships.

Jealousy, insecurity, loneliness, financial mismanagement and other negative feelings and behaviors can all rear their ugly heads in this setting. If a couple has not expected that graduate school may contribute to these feelings and has not made the commitment to work through any of these things that may come up, it can be devastating to the relationship.

The Story of Kim and Donnie

Kim and Donnie felt the effects of graduate school and reluctantly ended a 3-year relationship that both admitted had been very good. At the end of college, Donnie went into the Army and Kim went to graduate school. Both of them were in totally new places where they knew only a few people related to either the military or the grad school. They had been very close and had always felt that they were each other's best friends.

The distance created many lonely nights and extremely expensive telephone bills, to which Kim could not contribute. Also, because she was not employed, except for her research stipend, she could not afford to pay for the constant air travel as they tried to see each other often at first. She felt bad because Donnie was paying for everything. Also, although Donnie's military requirements were taxing, he had a lot more free time than did Kim. As her cards and letters became less frequent, and she did not have the time to visit as often, Donnie felt neglected and deserted.

After a time, phone calls and visits turned into arguments and shouting matches. They managed to struggle through the 2 years and Kim got her master's degree. She had been an excellent student and her mentor had encouraged her to apply to doctoral programs. She was accepted to several and was offered the necessary financial support. Unfortunately, another 3 to 4 years of a doctoral program didn't mesh with Donnie's military assignments. When faced with the option of a continued long-distance relationship, Donnie said he had had enough. Kim would have to choose. She wanted to get her doctorate, so they broke up.

Lovers Leaving: A Common Occurrence

There are many documented stories out there of people who lose a lover in the middle of the dissertation process and have their dissertations delayed by a year, or they never finish. Accounts of not being able to eat or sleep, and definitely not being able to concentrate, are common in these types of endings. Students are under a great deal of stress, may have financial worries, and are sometimes dependent on a spouse or lover for emotional support. Then, if the lover leaves, it feels as if the whole world is crashing in.

A friend of mine who went through it said he felt as if "someone had ripped open my chest and pulled my heart out with their bare hands." He was working on his dissertation, in the last 2 weeks of interviewing subjects for his study, when *the letter* came. His girlfriend informed him that she had found someone new. When he tried to call her, she didn't answer and would not return his calls. He stumbled through the last few interviews and just laid around his apartment with no energy or motivation. A month passed, and he just laid around. He decided to visit his sister in another city over the holidays and he called to tell me he was taking a semester off to get his head together. According to him, he could work in his sister's business for a few months, get over it, and pick right back up where he left off on his dissertation. I hope he eventually finishes.

Making Relationships Work in Graduate School

Relationships are hard in graduate school and there is not a foolproof remedy for how to keep your relationships on track during graduate school, but here are some ideas.

• Discuss all aspects of graduate school at length with your partner. If possible, take your partner with you to information meetings and campus visits. Have open and frank conversations about what will be required and the time, energy, and resources (particularly money) necessary to complete the degree. Ask him or her to make a firm commitment of support. If the partner will not, and you choose to go on to graduate school anyway, at least you know up front not to count on him or her.

• Sit with your partner and make a "safety plan." This plan is for the safety of your relationship and is a proactive approach to how you will resolve feelings of rejection, loneliness, and other problems that may arise. Also, be sure to talk about how you will celebrate the accomplishments and milestones. This can be a fabulous incentive program for both. One example might be, "When you pass your orals, we are going to Jamaica for a long weekend" or "When I pass my orals, I am sending you away for a golf weekend." Establish a consistent time for evaluating your plan so that either person does not feel guilty and more stressed for having to admit that the plan is not working.

• Work hard to let your partner know that despite the time involved in the graduate process, he or she is loved and is a priority in your life. Set up a routine for how you will make contact, but don't *be* routine in how you show your love. Ask each day, "What have I done today to show my partner that I care?" Leave a handmade card on the pillow. Slip a love letter in his or her briefcase. Leave a message on the answering machine. Pack a picnic lunch. Run a hot bath. I think you get the idea that there are a number of small things that you can do that mean a great deal.

• Talking increases intimacy. Don't be afraid to talk about your hopes, dreams, and fears. Don't shut out your partner. Ask for and give hugs. Cuddle. Learn how or remember to be romantic. And most of all, don't give up sex just because you are in graduate school. (Most parents should skip this next part.) Students tell me all the time, trying to make me feel guilty I'm sure, that because of the rigors of graduate school, their sex life has been on the downhill slide. The response in my head that I wish I could say aloud is that they might do a little better in class if they have a little fun the night before. Their disposition certainly might be more pleasing. This assumes that the research on the benefits of having sex is valid and reliable. I'll let you be the judge of that.

• Develop friendships to have some of your needs met outside the relationship. Not the particular one that I discussed a few sentences ago however. This may be a problem if your partner finds out. And, according to my mother and probably yours, sooner or later the partner will find out because "What you do in the dark will come to the light." The echoes of that line kept me out of trouble many days. Seriously though, it is unrealistic to expect your spouse, significant other, or partner to meet all of your needs. Supportive friends are important and necessary.

• Stay positive and see this degree as a benefit for you *and* your relationship. A friend of mine, Byron Greene, has a wonderful way of putting it. "You got a good thing, I got a good thing, and together we make a better thing."

• If you have children, don't forget to include them in the special attention that you give to your family.

IF THE RELATIONSHIP MUST END
WHILE YOU ARE IN GRADUATE SCHOOL

Sometimes, even with all you do, a dissolution of the relationship is necessary. It's just not coming together. Students say, "I'm in a horrible relationship and it is really working against me as I try to get this degree." They want out, but they are afraid to experience the pain of the breakup and go through the graduate process alone. A situation such as this requires a choice, pure and simple. Is the pain deeper in the relationship, or is the pain deeper outside the relationship? Do you really need someone who can't be supportive and meet your needs? Do you love yourself enough to believe that you deserve the best? Answer the question and go on from there.

Dr. Kennedy Schultz, founder of the Atlanta Church of Religious Science, has given countless numbers of people the following affirmation: "I can never lose anything that is necessary for my greater good. Any person, place, or thing leaving my life is making room for the greater and the better, and I am open and receptive." The translation is, if you have to move someone out of your life so that you can be your best, don't worry that you will be alone, because every person or thing that you need to support you in improving yourself will be provided.

Remember that relationships are important, a dissolution of one can be a major loss, and losses are painful. A grieving process is required before the healing can begin. Don't let anger and grief set in, paralyzing you. Do what it takes to turn the loss around and make it an asset instead of a liability. Be one of those people that get the "I'll show you" attitude and go after your goals. A highly recommended book for dealing with relationship losses is *How to Survive the Loss of a Love* (Melba Colgrove, Harold Bloomfield, & Peter McWilliams, 1991).

FINDING A LOVE

The second most important concern that the recent graduate school survivors mentioned was finding someone with whom to be in a relationship while in graduate school. Female students especially noted that they had a more difficult time finding eligible African American men to be involved with. Students said that they were looking for mates who were well-educated, caring, considerate, stable, honest, attractive, outgoing, liked to travel, had developed long-term, self-improvement goals, and were interested in upward mobility. Most of us would agree that these are reasonable expectations for a mate.

I've conducted workshops for several years on the topic of relationships and finding a mate, and I think the instructions are generally the same for graduate students and anyone else interested in having an intimate relationship.

1. Clean up your "stuff." Get rid of the personal baggage that you have been carrying around from things that have happened in your childhood and in previous relationships. If you are looking for someone to make a fresh start with, so are they.

2. Practice loving yourself and others in preparation for that special person.

3. First, become the person that you are looking for. If you want someone loving, kind, compassionate, and honest, then become those things yourself.

4. Be clear about the qualities in a person that you are looking for. List the special attributes that are important to you. Decide which ones are negotiable and which are not. Don't settle for anyone just to keep from being alone.

5. Get out to places where you might meet people: library, church, a friend's home, community action meeting, theater, gym, concert, tennis courts, other sporting events.

6. Be patient and enjoy life with yourself until the special person comes along. Being desperate is a *major* turnoff.

Several people have asked that the question of dating someone different from you be addressed. That really is a personal decision based on one's own philosophy or ideology, but I will offer the following insights based on my experience in the graduate school setting as a student and now as a professor.

• As a general rule, dating one of your professors is usually risky business. If the relationship turns sour, you can get burned, because grading can be such a subjective thing.

• Date someone who has an understanding of what academia is all about. Someone who knows what you are going through is less likely to be insecure and demanding when you have to study or work on projects.

• If you are a doctoral candidate and expect to be in circles complementary to your degree, look for someone who can hold his or her own and not be intimidated by these folks. For instance, a friend of mine never goes to social functions related to her job, because her husband says he feels uncomfortable around people with doctorates. Her lack of attendance makes her feel isolated and out of the loop, because lots of information is passed on, ideas are planted, and decisions are sparked at informal social gatherings.

SAFE SEX

In this day and time, we should not have to mention this topic as essential. We know that it is. So, as a reminder: *Practice safe sex.* Men and women can be as flaky in graduate school as anywhere else. Graduate schools do not necessarily make nice people, just ones with degrees. Take responsibility for taking care of yourself. Protect yourself and your partner *every time.*

BALANCE AND SELF-LOVE ARE KEY

In summary, this entire chapter "boils down to" two things: taking care of yourself and having the right mix of ingredients for success. First, loving yourself more than anyone else will ever love you is a must for survival. And when you love yourself, you *will* take care of yourself and your commitments.

Second, balance is essential, everything in moderation. Graduate school survivors excel academically and personally when there is a right mix of study, rest, play, contemplation, social activity, and recreation. We are people first and then scholars. Our goal is to be healthy and whole, not remnants of too much of anything.

6

A HANDBOOK FOR
MASTERING THE MOVES

Any good athlete, writer, musician, orator, or craftsperson will tell you that to win or be at the top of your field requires mastery of certain techniques and concepts. You have to know what works, the theory behind what works, how to use the technique well, and be willing to take risks.

A few months ago, I met an accomplished entrepreneur and self-made rich man, Marion "Duke" Green Jr. He is quite an interesting character: intelligent, articulate, outgoing, charming, flamboyant, confident, *and* very business savvy. As I watched him maneuver and listened to him talk about his road to wealth and business clout, I noticed several things. First, he is very creative in the ideas that he generates. However, his creativity is grounded in the knowledge of the rules of the game and how to level the playing field. He is politically astute and does his homework. Second, he assesses his strengths, maximizes them, and surrounds himself with talented people who bring the skills he needs and work well with his strengths. He has fine-tuned the moves necessary in his field, and he is smooth. Third, he takes calculated risks and lots of them. Recently he joined his wife's architectural and engineering firm, making the move from the computer software design business. This is what he said, responding to the move (personal communication, September, 1996).

Joining the architectural and engineering firm after 30 years as an entrepreneur in the computer software design business obviously places me in a new and different environment. What is not new, however, are the basics of operating a successful business and the ability to transfer these skills. Here, then, is how I envision helping to catapult this dynamic firm into improved earnings and growth.

Get the message: it's about mastering the moves.

Speaking of mastering the moves, let's talk about his wife Deryl's architectural and engineering firm in Washington, D.C., McKissack and McKissack. She is no "lightweight" either. The Washington-based firm of McKissack and McKissack, separately owned by Deryl, evolved from a strong lineage of architects who proved through their phenomenal track record that they understood the keys to success.

The first McKissack was a young man brought from the Ashanti tribe in Ghana, West Africa and sold into bondage in North Carolina. Through his courage and determination, he became a master builder and it was his mastery of this trade that allowed him the freedom from slavery. He passed his trade down to his son and grandson and their sons. Eventually, two McKissack brothers were the first registered architects in the state of Tennessee. Their lists of accomplishments were incredible, including the $5,700,000 contract to build the 99th Pursuit Squadron Air Base at Tuskegee, Alabama. This was the largest contract ever awarded to an African American firm by the U.S. government at that time and the list does not end there.

The firm then was passed on to William DeBerry McKissack, the youngest son of one of the brothers, who took the firm to still greater heights with international contracts and projects. Upon his retirement, his wife Leatrice took the reins of the firm as CEO and the growth continued.

Just as one begins to wonder whether the legacy will continue or if there are any more sons, in step three daughters all firmly established in the family business in four locations around the country. To date, Deryl's firm has provided services to such clients as Georgetown University, Howard University, The Urban Institute, the American Bankers Association, Mercer Management, AT&T, The United Negro College Fund, George Washington University, University of Maryland Medical System, The Injured Workers Insurance Fund, SIGNET Bank, Crestar Bank, Congressional Black Caucus Foundation, and federal, state, and city government agencies (information courtesy of McKissack & McKissack, personal communication, September, 1996). And the list is still growing.

The message for African American scholars through the success of these two African American entrepreneurs and their family legacy is that you must master the skills of winning. Graduate school requires a scientific application of techniques and skills. These "moves" increase the probability of successful completion.

MOVES TO SUCCESS

▨ Good Study Tactics

1. Find a place that is comfortable, free of distractions, and conducive to learning. Generally, don't use your bed, because it sends your brain the message that bed is for sleeping. So, your brain doesn't take you seriously when you say you want to study and sends back the signal to do what you normally do in bed, *sleep*.

2. Plan your study time based on the specifics of each course. Make actual appointments to study on your calendar.

3. Read as much as you can as often as you can. Don't wait until it is time for the exam or the paper to start reading. Read something each day except on your day off.

4. Write down the material while you are studying. Seeing the information in your own handwriting will help trigger your memory later.

5. Seek other sources to complement and clarify your texts and assigned readings.

6. Focus your attention on understanding the concepts presented and how they are operationalized. Though the amount of memorization of information varies, depending on fields of study, the expectation is that graduate students will be able to apply concepts, not just memorize and regurgitate facts.

7. Whenever possible, become a member of a reliable, serious, study group. Rule of thumb: Avoid study groups in which most of the people know less than you.

▨ Useful Test-Taking Strategies

1. Attempt to identify the format of the examination. If it will be composed of multiple-choice, true-false, or fill-in-the-blanks, you should plan to know more detailed facts. If the exam will be of the

essay nature, be prepared to discuss issues and analyze key points. Then use detailed information to flesh out ideas and anchor your statements. Expect the majority of exams in grad school to be essay.

2. Rather than agonize over what you think the test will be like, go directly to the source. In a productive way, ask the professor about the important focal points.

3. Don't wait until the last minute to read the material. Reserve time each day to review notes and process information.

4. Create a list of possible exam questions. Prepare them as thoroughly as possible, but explore more than one element of a particular question.

5. Get a good night's rest before the exam. Fatigue decreases the ability to trigger your memory.

Writing Papers That Work

1. Whenever possible, choose topics that meet the requirements of the course and fit into your master plan.

2. It's okay to build on papers and ideas on which you have previously written, but don't turn in papers that you have written for other classes. It's amazing how many students think they are fooling professors. Professors are fairly astute and they do talk to each other.

3. Review the basics of English composition, such as making outlines, developing strong topic sentences, and so forth.

4. Use the standard techniques of composition and the requirements of your field to construct your work. Consult the specific guide that shows you how to write in your area. For example, a guide to the American Psychological Association (APA) format is used in the social and behavioral sciences. See your bookstore.

5. Be sure to check your grammar, spelling, and punctuation. If you need help, most colleges and universities have special assistance available in this area. Don't be embarrassed about seeking help. You'll feel less embarrassed getting help than receiving poor grades on all of your papers.

6. Edit your work carefully, or get someone reliable to edit it for you.

7. Don't wait until the last minute; for most, it shows.

8. Get a *computer and printer* of your own if at all possible. It does not have to be the most expensive one in the store, but make sure that you can access the Internet and check or send electronic mail. Take a computer orientation class to learn about all of the amazing

information and the time that can be saved through technology. Learn to use software spell checkers and grammar checkers.

■   Developing Your Public-Speaking Skills

1. Realize that effective public speaking is integral to most careers. You will have your fair share of it as a graduate student, so don't shy away from it. Public speaking is not something to fear but to master.

2. Give special attention to developing your skills. One of the most successful, inexpensive organizations, and a really great program for building skills and confidence in public speaking, is Toastmasters. The organizations are available in many cities and serve as teachers and supports. Two great things about a Toastmasters organization, as opposed to taking a course on campus, are the lack of academic pressure and the fact that it is ongoing.

3. Attend public-speaking seminars.

4. Study and emulate the habits of people whom you consider good public speakers.

5. Practice by making presentations in your courses, at special meetings, and in community forums. Whenever possible, sit on panels and present papers at conferences. This kills two birds with one stone—you get the practice and the exposure.

■   Integrating Our Creativity and Cultural Heritage

1. If you are going to represent Afrocentrism in your speech, dress, papers, and presentations, make sure you know our history and cultural heritage because someone *will* call you on it. Graduate school is the kind of place where classes and programs often challenge our values and philosophies.

2. Don't be afraid to use colors, information, stories, and other parts of our culture to creatively display ideas and thoughts when appropriate.

3. Avoid being seen as one-dimensional. In other words, if someone were to ask members of your class who you were, ensure that they will describe you as more than just "the black student."

4. Use the principles of Kwanza as a guide for helping you maneuver the graduate school game.

5. Whether you attend a black institution or a white one, don't lean on the color of your skin as a crutch. It does us all a disservice.

6. Believe in solidarity, but don't feel responsible for speaking and acting on behalf of every person of color. Respect the individuality in the way that each person experiences graduate school.

Making Connections and Picking Your Battles

1. Get out and meet people who have expertise to share and may be helpful to your development.

2. Attend conferences and meetings where there will be people you want to connect with. This is an excellent way to network.

3. Keep a file and maintain contact with people that you meet. Ask them to introduce you to other people they know.

4. Run for office as a student representative in state and national organizations.

5. When it comes to getting involved in controversial issues, remember that your primary focus is to get the degree. Don't stick your head in the sand, but choose carefully which issues you will support or defend. Always be true to your ethics and principles, but learn to stay out of personal battles that do not serve your best interest. Case in point: You make an "A" on a paper, your friend makes a "C." You really thought it should have been an "A," so you allow your friend to use your paper to compare his against. The professor rereads your paper. Now, you get a "C" too. Other alternatives for supporting a friend?

6. As a rule, stay out of other people's business. You have enough stuff to keep up with trying to finish your own degree.

General Classroom and Meetings Etiquette

1. Be on time for classes and meetings. Not only is being late disruptive to the class, but it points you out as too scattered, unreliable, or uninterested. Neither of these adjectives will get you selected for special projects nor monetary awards.

2. Bring the proper books and materials with you. It's embarrassing to have to look on with someone for every handout the professor discusses.

3. Sit properly and act as if you are fascinated by the subject material and the professor's presentation. Even if you are bored, suffer through it. Though most professors are not vindictive, they do remember the students who sleep, doodle, read other articles, or write letters during their classes. I am continually amazed by students' lack of

perception about how far the professor's vision actually ranges and by graduate students who think that adjusting their daily organizers is acceptable classroom behavior. Graduate school is an adult learning milieu, but there are still norms and expectations for appropriate behavior.

4. Be prepared to participate meaningfully in class discussions and meetings. Silent students often blend into the crowd. At the undergraduate level, silent students may be noticed because they make good grades, but in graduate school almost everyone makes good grades.

MASTERING ONE OF THE BIGGEST MOVES OF ALL: THE COMPREHENSIVE EXAMINATIONS!

The key to mastering either the comprehensive or oral examination (comps) is preparation that is consistent and ongoing. Begin to prepare for your comps with your first course. Most programs begin with a foundation year or period, and this is normally the introduction to the field. In these courses, you will generally get content and readings that discuss the important theories, processes, and scholars in the field. It is important to read and assimilate as much of the literature and research as you can. The advanced courses build on these. You must know the literature to do well on oral and comprehensive exams.

At the end of each course, make an appointment with the professor and ask about the topically related questions from the class that one may expect to find on the comprehensive or oral exams. This is a valuable practice because generally the professors in each department construct the exam questions. So, if you do this with each professor, you will have all of the bases covered.

Oral exams are a bit tricky because professors are questioning you aloud. The same preparation is required along with a strategy of understanding the question and thinking carefully about the answer before proceeding. Again, preparation and practice are the keys. For a detailed discussion on successfully surviving the "oral interrogations" of graduate school, see the chapter on thesis or dissertation defense.

Establish study groups as early as possible with people who will be taking exams at the same time. Check to see if the department will provide sample questions from previous exams and ask former students what were their exam questions.

Comprehensive exams are usually just what the word means and they cover a wide expanse of the subject information. Rossman (1995) has a nice chapter on preparing to pass one's comps, which I recommend.

IT'S NO SECRET

To succeed at graduate school you need a number of resources. Nevertheless, none of the resources are more important than the ones you create for and within yourself by mastering the necessary skills so that you control the process instead of it controlling you.

7

Selecting and Managing Your Major Professor and Advisory Committee

THE MAJOR PROFESSOR

One of the most significant decisions any doctoral or master's candidate must make is the selection of the major professor. The major professor serves many roles, some of the most crucial being guide, mentor, editor, critic, advocate, and expert. It is the major professor's job to "get you through" the thesis, dissertation, the dissertation defense and, usually, the comprehensive and oral exams. A good major professor will steer you through the doctoral process by providing the necessary guidance for developing your plan, technical assistance, troubleshooting, running interference with other committee members, helping you to stay focused, and generally helping you to avoid as many pitfalls and obstacles as possible. A good major professor is not one that will "just let you take all of the bumps and bruises and see how you stand up!"

Most programs require that a major professor be selected by the time a student is ready to be admitted to candidacy in a doctoral program or by the second year if a student is in a master's program. There is usually a formal process by which the school or university is notified of the student's choice. Any changes must be made through the same notification process.

Though this chapter primarily references the process for the doctoral student, the information is very similar for the master's student, so it will not be duplicated in a separate chapter. The major difference between the two is the number of committee members.

A good rule of thumb is to start looking for potential candidates for the major professor at the beginning of your program. The selection of the major professor should not be a quick or impulsive decision based on limited facts. Don't wait until the last minute to pick someone that you don't know very much about. Also, it is helpful to identify this person early so that you have continuity and support through your comprehensive and oral exams. Too much of your success or ease in completing the degree depends on the student-major professor relationship. Begin building a relationship early with at least three people that you think may be good choices for major professor. After you have made your choice, and if the other two are still good candidates, then put the other two on your committee. Obviously, an easy way to begin the process is to evaluate the professors that you have classes or seminars with. Typically, this will expose the student only to a small number of faculty members, so students must methodically seek to meet and become involved with other faculty members in the school or department. The question often arises about choosing a major professor from another department or outside the school, but this is usually not allowed by many departments unless there is a cooperative agreement. So, in most cases, forget about bringing in some prolific scholar who went to school with your mom and dad, good friend, cousin, or outside consultant to direct your dissertation process.

The most important thing to remember here is that your major professor should be someone whom you know and will feel comfortable working with. I cannot stress this point enough. If one analyzes the *Education Digest* (National Center for Education Statistics, 1995) statistics over a number of years, the commonly made statement that "50% of all African Americans who complete the course work, pass the exams, and officially get ABD status never get the degree" seems true. They don't finish the dissertation! What a waste!

As an African American professor at a predominantly white university, I am often confronted with the question of whether African American students should strive to select major professors of color. The obvious answers for some may be yes, of course, or no. Would we all vote for a black political candidate just because he or she is black? Either answer may seem cut-and-dried, but this is really a tough call. At the risk of being called something less than a "homegirl," let me explain. Senior-level (associate or full), tenured, African American faculty members may make great choices for major professors if they meet certain criteria that we will discuss a bit later. Unfortunately, in many colleges and universities there are very few of these faculty members. In fact, in the department where I received my doctorate, there were no black faculty members, period. Sometimes the pool of African American senior faculty candidates may be too small to select a major professor who will be a good match for you.

On the other hand, because of the recent hiring of African American academics at many colleges and universities, students may have access to a larger number of junior, untenured black faculty members. This larger pool of African American academics still may not be the safe haven that doctoral candidates are looking for. First, it is very difficult to orchestrate the dissertation committee, which is likely to have several tenured members, without one being tenured him or herself. Most untenured junior professors are always trying to walk the line between being true to themselves and playing the game for promotion and tenure, which in many cases sometimes feels like a broader extension of the dissertation process. Most untenured junior professors are not able to wield wide-sweeping powers to convince, sway, or overrule more senior, tenured professors who serve on committees and may want to leave their mark on a particular student's research. The bottom line is that junior professors wanting to be promoted and tenured are not looking to alienate people who will vote on them. This fact alone makes serving as a major professor tenuous at best for any junior African American faculty member.

Also, African American junior faculty members are usually very busy establishing their own records of scholarship, teaching, and serving as mentors for students. They often serve on many departmental, school, university, and community committees, and many have administrative and normal faculty duties. We might describe them as having to be all things to all people but not at a point in their careers to be the most effective major professors.

Having survived the process, many of my African American colleagues and I have had many conversations about the characteristics one might look for in selecting a major professor. Here are the top 10. Nevertheless, you should know that we could not all agree on the order. A candidate for major professor should

1. Be well respected by his or her peers and command the authority and expertise to get you through the process. A major professor should not be someone who everyone else is "out to get." You may be the one caught in the cross fire.
2. Be an advocate for you—in your corner through thick and thin;
3. Have time and the desire to be integrally involved in your graduate school process;
4. Be connected in the department, school, university, and community to resources and colleagues with expertise that you can avail;
5. Be able to clearly articulate the expectations of the doctoral process and how to meet them;
6. Have an interest in and a minimal working knowledge of your topic;
7. Be willing and capable of providing technical assistance, structure and deadlines. In many life situations, autonomy is great, but structure is better for surviving the doctoral process. This is not the time to be left alone to find your own way.
8. Do not see your exam and dissertation process as a favor that he or she is doing for you;
9. Be healed from his or her own dissertation process; close enough to still remind you of the dangers and pitfalls but far enough away not to transfer personal feelings from that process to yours;
10. Be someone who will go the extra mile to "get you through" because he or she believes you are worthy of the title of "Doctor."

THE ADVISORY COMMITTEE

Once you have selected your major professor, the next step is to select your advisory committee. The committee is typically composed of three to five members who approve or disapprove of your dissertation title, dissertation prospectus, and ultimately the dissertation. The master's advisory committee has similar duties. At this juncture of your academic career, you answer to these five (or so) people. Many have tried to go their own way with the dissertation only to receive a wake-up call (or should I say a wake-up bomb!) from their committee. Though you are the master of your own fate, whether you pass or fail ultimately lies with these five people. They serve as experts, critics, judges, pseudoparents, and, if you pick the right ones, supporters.

Many students make mistakes by handling the important tasks of choosing a major professor and committee in the exact opposite way described here. They solicit members of their committee first and then select a major professor. This often puts the major professor and student at a disadvantage, because the major professor then may be forced to work with colleagues who are not a match for the project. Remember, it is the primary job of the major professor to "get you through," so you almost always have a smoother ride if your major professor has significant input regarding who is on your committee. Typically, your major professor will suggest people with whom he or she has worked before and share a similar philosophy about the doctoral process. Doctoral candidates may want to have people on their committees who are important to them because they have engaged in a particular type research or were good classroom instructors or community leaders. These are all great criteria, but the bottom line is, will these people all get along with each other? Whether these people can come together as a team is the crucial question. If your committee is fighting and ego-tripping, you are the one who gets caught. I'm not suggesting that you abdicate all authority for choosing your committee to your major professor, but I am strongly recommending that this be a joint venture.

A Sister's Committee Memories

Not too long ago, I was making a presentation on graduate school, and I met an African American sister who had recently gotten her PhD. Because neither one of us really knew anyone else at the meeting, we decided to have lunch and just hang out for a while. We started off with the cursory kind of academic and formal conversations that we had gotten used to in our professional settings, acting like we were at the West Palm Beach Garden Club (I know you know what I mean). But, when we got around to talking about our doctoral experiences, it was like Mary Jane Blige and Queen Latifah at the beauty shop. We whooped!

The sister told me that she had had at least three different committees because the folks couldn't get along. Her first two committees couldn't agree on anything. One professor would say "put this in"; another would say take it out. There were all kinds of stuff going on, racial issues, gender issues, egos, you name it, and it showed up at her committee. Her initial mistake was that she had asked five members to serve without designating a major professor first and at least three of the five had just assumed that they would be the major professor. The fighting began from that moment on. If one professor knew something about a subject, the other knew more. Each was pulling her aside to talk about everybody else. It was a mess.

Finally, two people dropped off, because of a new position at another school and a sabbatical, and she had to replace them. She selected two replacements from other departments on campus and ran the names past her major professor. He didn't know them personally but said to give them a try. So this became her second committee. As it turned out, one of the new people had previously dated one of the old members on the committee and had not amicably separated. Of course, it took her a while to find all of this out. They had too much baggage that was always the highlight of any committee meeting. Then, another professor got turned down for promotion and tenure, and he became angry and insecure. Soon it became apparent that she was going to have to disband this committee and start over if she ever intended to get this doctorate.

She fired two people, one person left, and she and her major professor picked three of his colleagues with whom she was somewhat familiar and, as it turns out, were interested in her topic. Though all this committee drama cost her an extra year, she learned some valuable lessons. Pick your major professor first. Listen to your major professor when he or she makes suggestions about who may be on your committee. He or she almost always has an ulterior motive. And if you have a good major professor, this agenda will usually work in your favor. If your committee isn't going to gel after giving it a sufficient run, get rid of it and start over.

THE COMMITTEE AS YOUR
CENTER OF EXPERTISE

Besides your committee being able to run like a well-oiled machine, it should also be your center of expertise. Use many of the same criteria in picking your committee that you used in picking your major professor, but begin adding individual expertise here. Visualize your committee much like a symphony, each member playing an integral part of the piece. See your major professor as the conductor of the orchestra, not as an expert on every instrument.

As a general rule, every committee should have at least one professor who has above average research capabilities and can take the lead in helping you develop the research design, analyze the data, and interpret the results. This person may or may not be the major professor. The research design and data analysis tend to be common problem areas throughout the dissertation and at the defense if they are not handled well up front. The advantage of having the guidance of a committee member in this area is that if problems do arise later, they become collegial issues between professors and not inadequacy on your part.

Having the research expertise on their committees may be particularly important for African American doctoral students who, like me, were educated in school systems years ago, which did not have mandatory research and statistics courses. As a result, many of us believed that these courses were meaninless and difficult and we avoided them at all costs. Subsequently, we arrived at graduate school feeling fearful and ill-prepared. Although we may have to take research and statistics in graduate school, the focus is usually on passing the courses and completing the requirement, not mastering the material for use at the thesis or dissertation phase. This is a common theme among students regardless of color. Rather than beating yourself up about your lack of preparation in the past, getting stressed out, and becoming immobilized by the fear, put a good, well-respected researcher on your committee and rely on his or her expertise. Usually, other committee members will follow that person's lead and you will short-circuit this as a major problem at the end.

Another important person to have on your committee is someone who has at least a moderate knowledge of your topic. You will need this person to help you define concepts and understand the variables that may have significant effects on your research. This committee member also will be crucial to the discussion chapter of your dissertation when you must explain what the results actually mean and whether they provide the answers you were seeking.

Include a good writer or editor on your committee. This professor helps you organize your thoughts and put them on paper in scholarly fashion. Look for someone who has a strong publication record in the major journals in your field. Learn not to take the comments and suggestions personally. Most people do not come to doctoral programs as highly published academic scholars and are not accustomed to writing in this format. I saved copies of each of my dissertation drafts and they were always all marked up. Some comments seemed picky and petty. I often thought it was just harassment—a major professor's job. Comparing many old drafts to the final product, I now realize the value of those editorial comments. Don't struggle about every little literary comment or change that may be marked on your manuscript. Don't see making the changes as a plot to stifle your creative talents. Just do it!

Finally, make sure that you have, at a minimum, one good motivator and head cheerleader. In addition to reading your materials and making comments, he or she ought to be someone who will pull you aside and say "don't give up, you've come too far."

I am continually amazed at the number of people who don't have someone like this on their committee. I didn't because no one ever sat me down and told me it was a good idea—part of the reason I'm writing this book. There were many things people didn't tell me. Anyway, there is a vast difference between having a motivator on your committee and not having one. Your friends, family, peers, significant other, and so forth all make good motivators, but most of them don't really know a thing about your dissertation except what you've told them. Don't get me wrong, their constant battle cries of "you can do it" is great. But, of course *they* would say you can do it, because they love you and don't really have a clue about what you are doing. Unless you've been through it, you don't understand the pressure, the guilt, the fatigue, the feelings of inadequacy . . . on and on. The truth of the matter is that you can do it, but sometimes that's hard to remember and you need to be pumped up by somebody who has been there, done that. A motivator on your committee not only knows the process but knows your research and realistically knows that it is possible to do *this* job. You can do it not only because you are competent but because the project itself can be done. Survivors of the process unanimously describe how important it is to have a motivator different from your major professor on your committee.

I think every doctoral candidate has heard the advice of just putting some "fillers" on your committee and I'm sure everyone may have contemplated it, even for a brief second. "Fillers" are those people who probably won't read the dissertation, won't suggest substantive changes, certainly won't put you on the spot by asking challenging questions at the defense, and, most important, will sign off on the dissertation. Okay, so I'm sure you're thinking, what's wrong with "fillers." First, you can't be sure who is really a "filler." Just because that was another student's experience with this person or 10 other experiences with this person doesn't mean it will be your experience. Maybe they like your topic and just might read yours. Second, "fillers" may move, retire, or die before you finish, leaving you with an empty spot on your committee. Will you be so lucky as to find another "filler?" Third, you don't have the benefit of maximizing this process as a learning experience, because at least one person is not making a significant contribution.

Don't worry about finding "fillers." If you used good criteria for choosing your committee members, you'll get a balanced committee. Each will focus on the same goal but will have different expectations and demands. Not all of them will be obsessive-compulsive, and not all of them will be totally laid-back. Sometimes despite your best efforts, you end up with a "filler." Then, count it all good and just go with the flow.

One of the most difficult things that a doctoral candidate may have to do is to ask a committee member to step down from the committee. The task itself may be unpleasant, but what the student worries about most is the possibility of retaliation. At the dissertation stage, there's not very much that a vindictive faculty member can do, provided that the major professor is supportive and the rest of your committee is solid and dedicated to your project. Even if that person served a crucial role, such as advanced researcher, you can still find another one. Don't be held hostage by having a person on your committee who impedes the progress of the entire group.

I have heard colleagues talk about being sexually harassed, coerced, and used by members of their committee because they thought they had to in order to finish. Frankly, you don't have to put up with it and you shouldn't. A friend of mine told me that one of her committee members always wanted to discuss her dissertation drafts over a late dinner somewhere. She felt that this woman was about to "come on" to her and it was really getting on her nerves and making her feel uncomfortable. When she asked my advice, I told her to stop being available during those hours and press for business hours. The professor became angry and passively aggressive, refused to show up for scheduled meetings and resorted to taking her anger out on my colleague's manuscript. After consulting with her major professor, she decided to ask her to resign from the committee. The initial incident was stressful, but in the end it was better than allowing that situation to continue.

Beware of the "prima donna" committee members who always act as if they are doing you a favor. The real deal is that university professors are expected to sit on committees. It's part of their jobs, fulfills their workload requirements, and it's mandatory in most places if they expect to get promoted to full professor. Favors go both ways. Also, look out for professors who rack up as many committees as the number of Denzel Washington movies in 1995 (seems like he was in a movie every month). Serving on committees takes time and you want to be sure that you're not one of the ones left out on the limb. There's nothing worse than trying to make a deadline, busting your butt to get a draft out for feedback, and having it sit on some professor's desk for 2 months.

While completing the process, it is not uncommon for committee members to accept jobs at other institutions, specialized fellowships, or sabbaticals, all of which may make them physically distant from you and the other members of the committee. Students often have to make the difficult decision of whether to keep these people on the committee and attempt to complete the work via mail, e-mail, conference calls, and flying back and forth. Most schools and universities have policies that specify conditions under which faculty members no longer employed at that institution may continue to serve on committees. For example, a major professor may take a new job at a different institution 2 months before a student is scheduled to defend her dissertation. It would be rather scary to get another major professor at this point, so this may be a good case for long-distance work. On the other hand, if a student is at a place in the process in which substantive drafts are being produced, a long-distance relationship with a committee member may be cumbersome. Assess the importance of that person's contribution, weigh the costs in terms of time, money, and convenience and make the decision to keep that person on your committee only if the benefits significantly outweigh the costs. Don't underestimate the amount of effort required to maintain a long-distance working relationship in completing the dissertation.

THE BOTTOM LINE

The bottom line is that your committee can play an integral role in making the process either exhilarating, bearable, or a living nightmare. Picking a good committee and implementing consistent but politically correct management requires proactive time and forethought. Better to put the work in on the front end than to suffer later. It's your call.

8

GETTING THROUGH THE
THESIS OR DISSERTATION

THE THESIS IS . . .

The thesis is an important requirement of many master's programs. Nevertheless, it is not mandatory for all persons receiving the master's degree. Whether it is required depends on the department. The thesis is a shorter facsimile of the dissertation. Often, the word *thesis* is used interchangeably with dissertation. In most cases, the thesis has the same expectations of original research and a contribution to the field as the dissertation. Information presented in this chapter is applicable to both the thesis and dissertation. Tasks and time lines given for the dissertation can be scaled down and used to complete the master's thesis.

THE DISSERTATION IS . . .

What is the doctoral dissertation? The doctoral dissertation is the single most important stand-alone requirement of almost all doctoral programs. According to Davis and Parker (1979),

> The doctoral dissertation is the documentation of independent research which makes a contribution to knowledge. Although there may be variations in the way different academic programs view the doctoral dissertation, the requirement appears generally aimed at achieving three objectives having to do with demonstrating the competence of the candidate to
>
> * do independent research,
> * make a contribution to knowledge with the research,
> * document the research and make it available to the scholarly community.
>
> The dissertation is both a documentation of the fact that the candidate has done independent research and of the contribution to knowledge. (p. xx)

Okay, so now that you understand what the objectives are, let me give you the real deal. The dissertation is a book. It is that black book with the gold writing on it that you see in all of your professors' offices. It's that black book that you see on the coffee table in the den in the home of the proud parents of many African American doctorates. As a matter of fact, my parents updated their den by taking down the gold clock with the pictures of John F. Kennedy and Martin Luther King on the side to make my dissertation the new centerpiece of the room. I did, in fact, feel honored.

The doctoral dissertation process is not like writing a "big" paper, and it doesn't compare to the course work or comprehensive exams. Though most academics won't admit it, besides all of the expectations that it be a scholarly contribution to the field and so on, it's an initiation. It's the proof that you deserve to wear the title "Doctor." It's a challenge. It's a test to see what you are made of, to see if you can "cut the mustard."

In years past, there was the rumor that the dissertation and the defense were designed to break you down. And professors were always looking for an opportunity to punish doctoral candidates for the way that they had been punished. I do believe this philosophy has moderated over the years, but it is still designed to be a very rigorous process. Though I do not support inhumane treatment, I can understand the need for rigor now that I've gone through the process (I couldn't make myself see the value of it while I was doing it). The doctorate is the terminal degree and it signals to the world that you are an academic expert in whatever field you have chosen. Being awarded the doctorate brings with it the expectation that you will be able to teach, lead, conduct research, and engage in scholarly thinking that will be important to the world. Not just anyone should be qualified to be called "Doctor." Once you've accomplished the goal of writing the dissertation and completing the degree, you have a special appreciation for anyone else who has gone through the process. You also realize how important it is as an African American to nurture others already in the process and to encourage more people to be interested in obtaining the doctorate.

So, why should you endure the dissertation? First, it is an important credential that can be used to help teach, empower, advocate, and make life better for others. Second, it will make you feel so good about yourself. Third, it is an accomplishment that puts you in a very elite "club." Some clubs are kind of nice.

Even with all the accolades, many people are put off by extreme fear regarding the dissertation. Let's put some of these on the table.

▓ The Five Most Common Fears About the Dissertation and Their Antidotes

I Am Not Smart Enough to Do a Dissertation! If you can read, write, follow instruction, complete a master's program, and pass doctoral courses, you are smart enough to do a dissertation. Review your accomplishments. Reread some of your old papers. Call a former or current professor who has been complimentary of your work for confirmation of your ability. There will be a bunch of people who can help you.

It Is Such a Massive Project That It Is Overwhelming! It *is* a big project, but the key is to do it one section at a time. Make a good plan and just work according to the plan.

I'll Never Finish! You will finish if you stay focused and persevere. See it as a game to be played and won. Thousands of other African American graduate students have successfully completed graduate school, and you can too.

I Have Heard That the Goal Is to Break You Down, and I Am Not Sure That I Can Handle That! There is no doubt that the process is rigorous. Sometimes it may even seem inhumane, but the goal is not to break you down. The goal is to attempt to ensure that you can make a contribution to knowledge through your research. Look at the dissertation as your proving ground. The higher the hurdle, the more pep in your step.

What If I Start the Dissertation and I Have to Take Some Time Off? Will the Requirements of the Program Prevent That? Most doctoral programs do have time constraints in which you must complete the dissertation. The average time that you have to complete the degree after entering candidacy is approximately 5 years. Though you would not want to break your momentum, conceivably you could take a couple of years off and still get it done on time. So, remind yourself that within reason, you do have some control over this process. Most programs *do* permit students to take formal leaves of absence.

THE DISSERTATION SCORECARD

▒ Length

Dissertations generally range in length from under 100 pages to 600 pages. The actual length will more than likely be based on the expectations of the major professor, type of research, and the appropriate format for research in your field.

▒ Time to Completion

The time spent working on a dissertation may range from several months to 10 or more years, but the average time to completion is approximately 24 months. The range is wide because some universities do not have a stipulation that the dissertation must be completed within a certain period. Nevertheless, most universities require that the dissertation be completed within 5 to 8 years of the student's reaching candidacy. If you anticipate that you will be on the "10 years and beyond" dissertation plan, it is best to look for a school without time requirements.

▒ Typical Stages in the Dissertation Process

The following stages are part of all dissertation processes:

Identify subject area for research

Select topic
Complete prospectus
Develop dissertation work plan
Perform literature review
Design and implement research instruments
Collect data
Analyze results
Write and edit dissertation drafts
Dissertation defense, corrections
Production of final version

Dissertation Format

There are several dissertation formats. As with the length of dissertations, specific formats are established by major professors and fields of study. For example, the social sciences may use "Format A" whereas the biological sciences may use "Format B." Therefore, it is not expedient to discuss each possible format. Nevertheless, as an example, a popular format for the social sciences is illustrated in Box 8.1.

Box 8.1. Dissertation Format

Front Pages
Chapter I   Introduction
Chapter II   Literature Review
Chapter III   Methodology
Chapter IV   Results or Findings
Chapter V   Discussion
References
Appendices

SELECTING THE DISSERTATION TOPIC

Begin looking for a topic when you contemplate attending a doctoral program. The nature of research that you are interested in may determine the field of study or the particular program or university that you select. Consider subjects that you are passionate about and that you feel will make a contribution to your chosen field and to knowledge as a whole. Think about subjects that you realistically can hope to answer specific questions about, because you must complete the research in a timely manner so that you can finish your dissertation.

The expectation of doctoral programs is that the dissertation fill gaps in the current knowledge base. One way to think about this is to develop a list of unanswered questions about a particular subject. The dissertation also may be a way to make clear subjects that are cloudy. Dissertations are often geared toward answering the question of why a certain phenomenon occurs or to formulate a list of causal factors at work in a situation.

Another way to enhance the success of selecting a good topic is to conduct a mini literature review by reading articles and other materials in your subject area for ideas. Talk to your major professor, other professors, and experts in the field about relevant topics. Students seeking topics may also contact organizations, such as public policy or economic "think tanks," to explore possible topics.

Last, consider topics that will offer career advancement. How does the dissertation fit into the "master plan" of your life? There has been considerable debate about whether African American researchers who write about African American topics are categorized as one-dimensional scholars, seen as scholars who are competent only in matters related to culture and ethnicity. For the student who may face this dilemma, one solution may be to select a cultural topic that has implications for other populations and makes a contribution to broader knowledge. Another very feasible solution is to go with your heart and write about subjects that inspire passion in you. This approach will often ensure that you are committed to the process. Though the dissertation is important, it is an early milestone in career development. The fact of the matter is that many doctorates go on to develop other interest areas and are often seen as experts in areas totally different from the dissertation.

THE DISSERTATION PROSPECTUS

The prospectus is the document that serves as the official blueprint of the dissertation. The prospectus is important because it is the detailed outline that guides your dissertation. It is akin to a building plan. No smart architect would erect a building without a plan.

The prospectus is written by the student and usually must be defended by the student before it is approved by the committee. In some programs, it is a formal process; in others, it is a more informal process. The defense of the prospectus is not as extensive as the dissertation defense, because the purpose of this defense is to provide helpful suggestions and guide the student in going about the research in the most effective way.

There are several ways to prepare the prospectus. The major professor and department will provide specific details. Most prospectuses will include the following components: a) brief introduction, b) detailed statement of the problem, c) need for the research, d) presentation of the research hypothesis, e) literature review, f) proposed methodology, g) anticipated outcomes, and h) a description of the dissertation chapters.

A detailed and accurate prospectus aids in writing the dissertation within the required time constraints and with as little trauma as possible. Time spent in the preparation and fine-tuning of the prospectus is time well spent. As you develop and refine your dissertation prospectus, the following summary points may be helpful:

Clearly define the problem or topic that prompted the need for research in this area.

Make sure that the topic is of value to the field. Get validation from people currently involved in the field.

Select a research project that can be finished in a timely manner so that you can finish your dissertation.

Evaluate whether the research hypothesis is clearly articulated and testable. If not, seek revisions.

Purchase a book specifically about writing the dissertation and consult the section on the prospectus.

Do not be threatened by the defense of your prospectus. Remember, the purpose of the defense is to fine-tune your prospectus, which will lead to a smoother dissertation process.

PLANNING THE WORK
OF THE DISSERTATION

One of the scariest things for most people when they think about getting the doctorate is whether they will be able to get the dissertation done. Once you get over the fear of not being intellectually capable of doing the work, there is still the anxiety of whether you can complete such a massive project in under 20 years, given that you would actually like to have a life during this time. Okay, 20 years is an exaggeration. Actually, it's a cruel joke I threw at you considering many programs may allow you only 5 years after reaching candidacy to finish the degree. Bottom line: Who wants to be working on this for all that time anyway? Second and real bottom line: Though you may be faced with terror and dread, you can get it done within your personal or required time line. The key is to make a plan and stick with it.

A plan for managing your dissertation is absolutely critical. For a project of this magnitude, you must have a road map. It should be an outline that details your work process step-by-step. It should include time, resources, places, dates, important events, and incentives. Make a good plan and then just work according to the plan. Probably 80% of all African American former doctoral candidates will tell you that the complexity of the content of the research was not the problem. The major problem in completing the dissertation was organization and perseverance. An initial organizational mistake can cost you as much as 6 months in time later in the process. And, it is very difficult to persevere if you feel like you are just going around in circles. It's like taking the local Greyhound from New York City to Los Angeles. To stay on that bus, you've got to either be going to get married to the only person you've ever loved, going to your rich uncle's funeral (thinking that you might be in the will), or be involved in some important social experiment, maybe your dissertation.

Steps in Making the Plan

One of the most important factors to consider when making your dissertation plan is to figure out how long you have to complete the dissertation. How long you have may depend on several factors, such as how much money you have, when your leave of absence is over, or when your family has said that time is up. Get honest with yourself and be realistic about what you're working with. As you are attempting to set a manageable time frame, make sure that you are setting goals that can be accomplished within your estimated time.

It would be nice to think that you can write a dissertation in 3 months, but the average is between 6 months and 1 year for people who put a full-time effort into the process. For many students, the process takes much longer because they often obtain employment while writing the dissertation. Because the course work is completed and money may be a concern, the decision may be made to go back to the workforce during the day and write the dissertation at night and on the weekends. I know that sometimes you "gotta do what you gotta do," but I caution against this if you have another option. To work all day and expect to come home at night and write a dissertation is a murderous ordeal at best. You are tired, stressed out, and this isn't even the worst of it. If being tired and stressed out aren't enough, try feeling guilty on top of all that. The dissertation can feel like an albatross hanging around your neck every moment of the day. No matter how much fun you have, it's overshadowed by knowing that you have this massive project that's got to be done. Working full-time can add another 2 to 5 years to the process. My advice and the generally agreed upon advice among doctorates: Tough it out for another 6 months or a year and focus full-time on getting the dissertation done. You'll be much happier and generally will have more options entering the field as a doctorate instead of an ABD.

As you make your plan, your time estimate should not only include writing time, but it must also include time for research, disseminating drafts and obtaining feedback, and any family or employment responsibilities. Be sure to factor in time for breaks and small vacations even if you just go away for a weekend. You will need to anticipate such delays as exhaustion, writer's block, and needing time to explore other relevant ideas that may come up during the course of your research. Don't try to do this dissertation without days off for rest and rejuvenation. It's almost impossible.

Here's another important tip when trying to figure out how long it will take. Ask your major professor what is an appropriate length for a dissertation. My major professor was very up front in offering his opinion that a good dissertation in my particular subject area could be written in 150 pages or less and that I should conform to those standards. That worked for me, considering that I had seen some dissertations that were 400 pages long. If there is one lesson I've learned in life it is that you can make some things a lot easier for yourself if you follow the directions. It's like being up until three o'clock on Christmas morning trying to put together the bike that Santa left only to discover that you could have been in bed by midnight if you hadn't used the sheet labeled "directions" as a coaster.

Another thing, be sure to include time in your plan to allow others to read and proof drafts of your paper for you. Friends and colleagues can be very helpful in this area, but they don't always operate on the same timetable as you do. Also, incorporate enough time to hire a reliable word processor if you can afford it. However, reliable is the operative word here. Turning a manuscript on a disk over to someone else to edit, correct copy, worry about the margins, and clean up the bibliography is almost euphoric. Being able to take care of these things yourself, because *you* have mastered word processing and your disciplinary bibliographic style sufficiently is even more empowering if you have the time and stamina. My advice is to word process your own work and hire someone else to clean up. In the long run it will save you time, money, and frustration, and in the process you will acquire a tremendously valuable professional skill.

Look at the timetable in Box 8.2 and 8.3 (the next page) and see if these will work for you. Make specific modifications that are important for your particular research, but don't forget to include time for rewards and incentives.

Box 8.2. Sample Dissertation Time Line

August	Preparation of detailed outline
September	Review of the literature
October	Conducting research
November	Conducting research and collecting data
December	Interpretation of results
January	Writing the dissertation
February	Writing the dissertation
March	Writing the dissertation
April	Editing and proofreading
May	Committee reviews draft
June	Revisions
July	Vacation and redistribute drafts
August	Revisions
September	Committee reviews draft
October	Preparation for defense
November	Dissertation defense

Box 8.3 Estimated Time for Dissertation Tasks

Preparing detailed outline of dissertation	40 hours
Review of the literature	15hrs/100 pages
Developing the data collection instrument	60 hours
Testing the instrument	20 hours
Collecting the data	120 hours
Analyzing the data	80 hours
Compiling the results	80 hours
Writing the dissertation	2hrs/page
Editing, rewriting, proofing	1hr/page
Preparing the summary and conclusions	4hrs/page

YOU NEED CASH OR CREDIT CARDS FOR THE DISSERTATION

Attention!! Attention!! Please be advised that the cost of your dissertation is not included in your tuition or fees. And sometimes the price tag is pretty hefty. Typical costs associated with the dissertation that you may have to pay for are

a. development of the topic via visits to research sites, telephone calls, and face-to-face interviews;
b. development of the research instrument;
c. reproduction of research materials;
d. supplies, xeroxing, postage, travel, telephone;
e. professional consultation;
f. assistance of a statistician;
g. word processing of drafts and tables;
h. production of slides, other visuals;
i. preparation of final draft;
j. university fees;
k. binding;
l. miscellaneous expenses.

These additional costs may range from $1,000 to $3,000, depending on the type of research and how much the student is able to do without hiring assistance.

WRITING THE DISSERTATION

▓ Making the Move to Get Started

Actually, just to think about writing the dissertation is an exhaustive endeavor. Whereas some say that writing the dissertation was a challenging experience and others say it was a miserable experience, they almost all agree on the fact that it can be very tiring and extremely stressful. For example, there was a recent newspaper story about an engineering student who shot and killed the members of his committee after they had rejected his dissertation. Reportedly, he had worked on his dissertation night and day for about a year and just snapped when he failed. Granted, this is not the story of every doctoral candidate but it does exemplify the time, energy, and personal emotion invested in completing the dissertation requirement.

As stated earlier, the process of writing the dissertation should begin at matriculation into the doctoral program. Papers, presentations, and conferences should be related to a potential dissertation topic. Go back and scan these things for ideas and themes to be incorporated into the dissertation. Look at the dissertation as an extension or the compilation of many other successful things that already have been done in your graduate school career. This is helpful because it allows you to start the process with a wealth of ideas to be explored and expanded.

Because the plan has been mapped out and the necessary information secured or identified, the next step is to just jump in, follow the plan, and start writing. Remember, the plan should require something to be written everyday, if nothing more than a paragraph. An interesting comment made by a professional writer is that no matter how gifted a person is and how beautifully his or her words flow, it takes practice to be able to communicate them on paper consistently. His sister shared with me what a struggle it was for him in the beginning of his career. He had been a very successful but unhappy corporate executive whose dream had always been to be a writer. He decided to make the leap and leave corporate America. This would be his livelihood, which meant that his family would continue to depend on him as a "breadwinner." At first it was great and he was sure that this was the right thing to do. Then, the "writer's blocks" and the desire to garden, paint (anything but write) came. He was soon forced to make a decision: Give up and go back to corporate America or see it through. He decided to see it through. He made an efficient office conducive for work that was his private space, and he made a work schedule every day Monday through Friday. Most important, he went to his office every day at his scheduled work time and sat in front of his computer to write. If something was flowing, he wrote; if not, he just sat there and looked at the computer from 9:00 to 5:00, with an hour for lunch and two 15-minute breaks. After a few days of this, things began to lift, and he started writing. Two major points here: He developed the discipline to stick with it and he trained his brain and body to automatically respond when he sat in front of his computer. You may not always write 30 pages every time you sit down or you may revise what you wrote later, but the point is that you write something. Personally, I used his technique and I have found that it does work. If you sit there long enough for enough days, you will write something.

Here is another hint: Some graduate schools allow students in selected disciplines (mostly the so-called hard sciences) to submit several published journal articles in lieu of a separate dissertation. See if that is possible in your department and consider it as one option to the conventional dissertation requirement.

What Should Be Written First?

What should be written first is an interesting question by itself. First things first, no pun intended. Having already written your dissertation prospectus, the groundwork for your introduction and literature review already should be well under way. So, write your literature review and introduction first.

Next, write the methodology and data collection chapter. The methodology chapter is important because it is in essence a blow-by-blow account of what you did to conduct your experiment or gather the information to support or reject the hypothesis based on the research question. Not only does it answer the question of what was done, but it also answers the question of why it was done in that way.

The methodology chapter is commonly a chapter that many people seek consultation on, because it is usually the most closely scrutinized chapter in the dissertation. Also, it is the chapter that a great majority of students feel the most insecure about. Almost all doctoral (as opposed to professional) programs have research course requirements. The research courses generally are designed to be instructive for the dissertation. But, many students come to the graduate research courses feeling scared and inadequate, because they did not have the exposure in their undergraduate experiences. Ditto for African American students. The objective of most students is to get through the research courses with their grade point averages intact and a promise to "really learn" the research before the dissertation rolls around. This is a very grand idea, but the fact is that they usually never get back around to learning that "research" before the dissertation. Who has the time? So, the moral of the story is: Try to really learn something about research in your research class. Nevertheless, should this plan fail, don't be afraid to ask for help in developing and documenting the methodology chapter. Ask your major professor, or someone else on your committee, or seek reliable outside help. Even if you think you have it under control, it is always a good idea to have your methodology chapter reviewed by someone competent in that area.

Get the introductory chapters (introduction, literature review, methodology) completed early so that the focus can be directed to the results and discussion portions of the dissertation. Evaluating solely on intensity of writing, except for the literature review, the results and discussion chapters may be the most taxing.

The next chapter to be written in the standard dissertation format is the "results" chapter. The final chapter, a discussion and interpretation of the results should be written last. Some doctoral candidates report that they jump around and write on different chapters out of sequence to break the boredom, but I would advise keeping this to a minimum.

Keeping Up With Your Stuff—Literally!

It is extremely important to establish a primary place to write. Not only should the space be conducive to getting work done, such as having a computer available, the proper lighting, and so forth, but it should also have adequate storage capacity. It is a good idea to have storage capability at your primary workstation and at a second location as well. Though not something that can be anticipated, it would be devastation on top of devastation to have your original data or a year's worth of work lost in a fire or flood.

Set up a storage system that includes files, boxes, and shelves specifically for your dissertation materials. Label all materials and when you finish with them at the end of the workday, put them in their proper places. Prepare your materials for the next day and position them so that they will be ready and accessible when you begin work. Procrastination kicks in and focus becomes fuzzy when you have to spend an hour at the beginning of your workday finding and organizing your materials.

Journals are efficient ways to jot down thoughts that you may want to explore in your work. Pick one that is small enough to take with you in your purse, pocket, or backpack. Whenever you have a significant thought, write it down. Tape recorders are also great tools for this activity and they can be used while driving. Some doctoral students have kept voice records of their work, including visits to the library, and have found it to be helpful. For example, rather than taking notes on various articles related to the topic, oral notes are recorded on tape.

Keep four copies of each draft that is produced: two hard copies and two on diskette. Label them as separate drafts: draft #1, # 2, or Chapter 1-1, Chapter 1-2. Store two of each draft (one hard copy, one on diskette) in your primary location and two of each draft (one hard copy, one on diskette) in your secondary storage location.

My mother often tells a story of going away to college in Virginia and seeing daily the campus legend, a late middle-aged man who suffered a psychotic break during the doctoral process. It seems that he was always spotted around campus going through the garbage cans mumbling about his dissertation. As the story goes, a couple of days before he was to turn in his dissertation that he had worked on for almost 10 years, it was stolen. No one knows whether it was stolen by someone who had planned to use it or whether it was just a cruel and malicious joke. He searched everywhere, even offered a reward, but it never turned up. Because this was in the 1930s to 1940s, there were no computers, and carbon paper was so cumbersome for a project of this length, this had been his only copy. He literally lost his mind and spent every day, until his health failed, looking for his dissertation. My mom vows that this is a true story and I can believe it, just remembering the anxiety I felt about carrying my diskettes around. Save yourself the experience of "high drama" by keeping more than one copy of each version of your draft.

Besides making copies of your drafts, make copies of all of your original data. Store copies of your data in two separate places as well. Copy other important materials, such as journal articles and interviews, also. I found it helpful to keep three sets of the articles with one in my briefcase so that I could read in any spare time that I had while waiting for appointments, and so forth.

One of the most important pieces of advice is: Back up your work on diskettes. Then, back up your diskettes. Then back up the backup diskettes. Save your work often. If you get up from the computer to get a drink of water, save your work. Most computer programs do have timed backups set at specific intervals, but you can still lose a couple of pages of crucial documents.

Technical Writing Tips

1. If you need help with your writing, don't let it paralyze you. Seek out people and other resources that can be helpful. Get a college grammar book. Ask a colleague or friend to assist you with editing. If you have the money, hire an editor to proof your work. Take a short creative writing class while you are in the data collection stage. In most fields, the dissertation is not considered creative writing, but the class may be the perfect vehicle to get your words flowing and break down any resistance to writing.

2. Purchase a book specifically on how to write the dissertation. They can be found at almost any college or university bookstore. A good book on this topic is one that describes the process in detail, step-by-step. One such book is *Writing the Doctoral Dissertation* (Davis & Parker, 1979); another is *Surviving the Dissertation* (Rudestam & Newton, 1992).

3. Learn the accepted way to document references and other special information specific to your field. Purchase a technical manual that will serve as a guidebook for any need that you may have. Your graduate school likely has a guide to the preparation of theses and dissertations. Get it, and follow it exactly!

4. As a way to stay grounded during the process, ask your major professor to help you develop a list of evaluative questions that can be answered each week. Sample questions are

a. What new information am I trying to add to the field through this research?

b. What is the overarching question that this research attempts to answer, such as "Do mentoring programs reduce teenage pregnancy?"

c. What are some specific questions to be addressed?
   "What kind of mentoring programs work best?"
   "Do the ages of the girls make a difference?"
   "What were other factors that may have affected the results?"

5. Write clearly and concisely. If you need help, one strategy is to identify a writing partner to discuss and review your writing. The purpose of the writing partnership is to avail another thinker who will

be knowledgeable about your work. Then, you reciprocate for that person.

6. Use proper English, correct grammar, and avoid slang or overly technical jargon.

7. Do your best to eliminate the use of the first person pronoun "I" (when I evaluated the data I found). Instead, say "the results of the data evaluation indicated."

8. Be careful about using such adverbs as "always" and "very."

9. Avoid the two "oses," grandiose and verbose. Don't use words that you don't need or understand to try to sound impressive or stretch out your dissertation. Both will be easily detected by your committee members.

10. Use subheadings to organize your thoughts and direct the reader's attention. Better to have too many at first than too few.

11. Use summary sentences at the end of each subsection to bring home your point. This is important. If you cannot write a clear and concise summary sentence at the end of each subsection, you probably do not have clear and concise writing in the section.

12. Set up a proofing system that allows you to put the document down for a few days and then come back to read it. Proofing a paper copy tends to be more accurate than using the screen.

13. The *b-i-g* tip, the mother of all mothers . . .

Do not wait until the last minute to write your dissertation. Forget about the time you stayed up all night and wrote the 30-page paper and got an "A" on it. It's not the same, trust me on this.

STAYING FOCUSED: YOU MUST PERSEVERE!

More than half the battle of getting the doctorate is to finish the dissertation. Though working on the dissertation can be an exciting, challenging, and exhilarating time, it is a time of exhaustion, great stress, and emotional turmoil. Sometimes the most predominant thought is to just give it up.

In a recent informal poll of African American doctorates, these are some of the statements they made.

"I wanted to just let it go!"

"I thought I couldn't write another word."

"Some days I would just sit and cry."

"My hair came out around the edges."

"I started gritting my teeth at night in my sleep."

As difficult as it may be to focus on the adversity in these words, the most important phrase in this paragraph is African American doctorates—people who made it. People who persevered.

Webster defined persevere as to continue in some effort, course of action despite difficulty; to persist. African Americans have a long history of perseverance. Stories of heroes and heroines, such as Harriet Tubman; Martin Luther King; Rosa Parks; and Osceola McCarty, a washerwoman from Mississippi, exemplify the concept of never giving up.

The dissertation is a true test of perseverance. It may be the closest many of us will know to what our ancestors experienced. When you are tired, keep going. When you are frustrated, keep going. When it appears that your committee will never think your work is perfect enough, keep going. When folks don't understand what you are going through, keep going. When your significant other starts acting crazy, keep going. No matter what, keep going.

Much Respect for the Man

I have a great deal of respect for a colleague and a strong black man by the name of Thelmon Larkin. I met this man several years ago when he first became a field instructor for graduate students doing internships. He is warm but firm, compassionate, consistent, intelligent, and dedicated. He has spent most of his career working in the juvenile court system trying to make a better way for kids in trouble. Through all of the hard work, unappreciative kids and parents, and a less-than-perfect system, he never lost the hope to believe that things could be better.

A few years ago, Thelmon started work on his doctorate to pursue a dream of university teaching. The road has been anything but easy. He has a family to take care of, employees and students to supervise, and many troubled youths to be concerned about. He balances working all day with being a father, husband, and scholar at night. No matter what, he keeps going. On many occasions he has contemplated whether it was worth it. On some of those occasions, he thought he should just give up. But he decided to keep going one more day, and one more day, and one more day. He has continued to persevere and is moving forward with the dissertation. I intend to continue supporting him until he finishes. I look forward to seeing Dr. Larkin in a classroom very soon.

In some ways, I think it is more difficult for African American men in the graduate school process, especially if they have assumed the financial responsibility for their families for many years. I also believe that the same hardship is present for single women supporting families and attending school and for persons with other physical or family challenges.

A woman from Alabama told me about the struggle she had battling lupus, trying to work full-time, and getting her doctorate in the health sciences field. No doubt it was a struggle. She related that she persevered, got to the homestretch, and had to hire someone to do the final word processor draft for her. She had gone on a trip and was to pick up the drafts, get them copied, and distribute them on the day she arrived home. She was cutting it close, but because of certain circumstances, she had to meet the deadline. The night before she was to return the following morning, her intuition and anxiety told her to call the typist and make sure everything was in order. The typist informed her that she had not even started the job; she thought the drafts would be picked up a few days later. This tired, courageous woman went off! She told the typist that the drafts had better be finished by 9:00 A.M. as they had agreed or she was going to drive her car through her living room window. I believe her exact words were "I am going to park outside of your house at 8:45 A.M. and if at 9:00 A.M. the door doesn't open with you bringing drafts, you *will* have a Volvo sitting in your living room. Not a threat but a promise." Of course I asked her if she really meant it, and at the time she said that she really did. Needless to say the drafts were ready.

When asked how they got the strength to persevere, a group of doctorates offered this advice.

• Stay tapped into your inner strength. Pray. Meditate. Whatever. Like Nike, whatever it is that you do, just do it and do it every day. Don't let up. Don't let any person, place, or thing steal from you the joy of living. Easier said than done, but this is a must.

• Take care of your body. A strong body is important to support your mental aptitude. When you are at peak performance, your mind is sharper. On the other hand, you may have a wealth of ideas, but if you are too tired or sick to work, they don't do much good.

• Schedule time for play. Have fun. Don't deprive yourself of all pleasurable activities just because you are working on the dissertation. The important thing is to work on self-discipline and stay focused.

• Take it day by day. Robert Ringer in *Million Dollar Habits* says that success is incremental, built one day at a time. One good day times seven becomes a good week, four good weeks become a good month.

Twelve good months become a good year. Simple but powerful advice if we can remember to use it. Focus on giving your best one day at a time. Live in the moment. Yesterday is over and tomorrow may not come. But, if you screwed up yesterday, you might have to pay for it today so keep the screwups at a minimum. It's hard trying to start today paying for yesterday; somewhat like the American Express Card. You can charge as much stuff as you want this month, but next month they want all of their money for the stuff you charged last month while you are still charging stuff this month that you have to pay for next month.

- Speaking of screwups, don't become paralyzed by them. Figure out what you have to do to fix them, forgive yourself for making mistakes, and move on.

- Have support systems. Note the word *systems*. You need more than one. Have an academic support system made up of professors and other scholars, have one with doctoral candidate colleagues, one with family and friends, and so forth.

- Celebrate your accomplishments each day. Smile. Hug yourself. Give yourself treats. Buy yourself flowers, leave yourself little notes on the PC or on the mirror. Call folks or send printed notes that say you have passed a certain milestone.

- If you need help dealing with fear, anxiety, or depression, don't sit there and let everything fall apart around you. Get it. You won't be the first or the last.

- Believe in yourself no matter what. Always remember who you are: a talented, competent, gifted, wonderful child of the universe who has come from a long line of kings and queens.

YOU CAN GET THROUGH

Every dissertation survivor has his or her own story to tell. Talk to other people and get theirs. Find out what made them persevere. For me, I had come too far, spent too much money, and had too many people depending on me—not just family and friends but several generations of young and old African Americans who need me as a role model and advocate. I stood tall for folks who also need me because I am an African American woman with a credential that commands respect. On the days when I thought I could not go on, I dug deep and realized that this was not just about me. It was about proving that in my field, a field dominated by white men, a black woman could do it and then reach back to make a difference.

9

SURVIVING THE DEFENSE

THE DISSERTATION DEFENSE

The dissertation defense is the final opportunity in the doctoral process for you to discuss and present your research and its intended contribution to the field. It is also the final opportunity for your committee to investigate the quality of your work and your ability to present it professionally under pressure. Many call it the last rite of initiation into the exclusive club of doctorates. The defense is usually part presentation, part thinking quickly on your feet, and part interrogation.

Over the course of doing research for this book, I contacted many former doctoral candidates, and most have one or two unforgettable memories about the dissertation defense. Either it was great or one of the worst experiences of their lives. There were few if any middle-of-the-road comments. One thing is for sure, they all said that preparation was the key.

PRELIMINARY PREPARATION FOR THE DEFENSE

One of the most important points to remember about defending your dissertation is that you are the expert on your research. In many instances, you may even be the expert on the broader subject, depending on who is on your committee. Take advantage of this. Too often doctoral candidates feel as if they are coming to the dissertation defense vulnerable and exposed. But, if you focus on the idea that no one knows your work better than you do, it provides you with confidence and a certain level of protection against the close scrutiny of your research by others who have already "gotten into the club."

A simple but costly mistake that many candidates make is that they don't go back and read the dissertation thoroughly before the defense. No matter how often you have previously read the manuscript and are convinced that you know the contents from cover to cover, it should be read immediately before the defense. When you have five others reading it and formulating questions for your responses, you will be surprised how much you may have forgotten or how obscure or asinine some of the questions can be. Remember, there are five different personalities on your committee and, from some stories I've heard, each has his or her own antennae for spotting significant things in your dissertation. The question is: significant to whom and why? You may not be able to answer every question, but at least you'll be familiar with what they are talking about.

Although rereading your dissertation may seem simple advice, sometimes it's very hard to do, not just because you think you know it so well but because actually you are sick of it. Sick and tired of reading it, working on it, proofing it, correcting it . . . just plain sick and tired of dealing with it. But, as much as you may feel emotionally and physically drained after completing the next-to-final draft, you've got to stay intimately involved with the document until after the defense.

Beyond reading your own document to prepare for the defense, you must read any current literature on your subject and be prepared to discuss the relationship of this new research to your work. Be particularly focused on research methodologically similar to yours and research that produced different results from yours. Analyze the strengths and weaknesses of the new work and the impact that you think it will make on the field. Incorporate this discussion assertively in your opening statement.

Most students complete their literature review at least one year before completing the dissertation and there may be other things regarding the subject matter published during that time.

The last thing you want to do is get caught with your "pants down" at the defense when some professor starts asking questions about what's new and "hot" in the field and you're still doing the "boogaloo." Now don't get me wrong, everyone should know how to do a good "boogaloo," but you need some James Brown "Get on Up" to get down and your committee might not be playing that song. Being out of touch at your dissertation defense is like going out on a blind date with a man who still wears burgundy polyester pants with a white belt.

GET A GAME PLAN FOR YOUR DEFENSE

Devise a strategy for your defense with your major professor. Inquire about the habits of the other committee members and attempt to get a feel for how they will conduct themselves in the dissertation defense. More than likely, your major professor has been on other committees with them and knows how they will act. It is your major professor's responsibility to solicit feedback from the committee members on the quality of the content in the draft before the actual defense. The major professor also should have some sense of the general sentiment of committee members on whether you stand a chance of passing. Sometimes, the feedback has been so negative that the major professor has canceled the defense knowing that the student would be "eaten alive" during the questioning.

Some major professors recommend that students meet with each individual committee member immediately before the defense, whereas others think that it is too confusing right at the end to get five sets of feedback. If you have a good major professor, follow his or her directive. In my case, my major professor's style was to have the responsibility of communicating with the committee members as opposed to me contacting them. The system was that I delivered all the copies of the draft to him and he distributed them to the committee. The feedback was to come directly to him and he would synthesize the information and relay it to me. As you might imagine, this style required that the student put a great deal of trust in the major professor, because in many ways you were isolated from your committee members down to the homestretch, and you saw their praises and criticisms of your work through your major professor's eyes.

I suppose that this can be a great system and can keep you focused at the end, but if this process breaks down it can be sheer hell. My advice is that during the period between distribution of the defense drafts and the actual defense, stay on your major professor. Make sure your major professor has read the draft and has actively solicited comments from the other committee members. Get as much information as you can, and do not sit back and let you and your major professor come to the defense unprepared.

I made the mistake of cruising to the defense thinking both my major professor and I were ready. I just assumed, because I had not gotten a telephone call from my major professor saying that the defense was canceled, it was pretty much a "done deal." As my grandmother used to say, "it's all over but the shoutin'!" This assumption about how dissertation defenses work is also a pretty common one on the rumor mill. Nevertheless, let me tell you from personal experience that this is not always the way it goes, and there is sometimes a lot of pain and high drama before it's all over.

Not having heard from my major professor since the drafts were sent out, I decided to call him a couple of days before the defense to see if he had any suggestions. Where was my head? I had not done any real preparation before then except to pull a few recent articles and scan my dissertation. My major professor told me to plan to make about a 30-minute presentation on the research, be ready to field questions, and stay calm. That was the extent of our conversation about preparation for the defense. So what did I do? Made some notes for my presentation, scanned a few articles, and browsed through my dissertation.

The reason for writing this book is to keep you from falling into the same traps. I was not prepared for what would happen in the defense. I had not done all of the things I am telling you to do. And, as thankful as I am to my major professor for getting me through, my dissertation defense was the worst academic or professional activity I have ever endured. True enough, I was not prepared primarily because of ignorance, but my major professor was not expecting that tone of the defense either. Because the other committee members had not sent him any specific memos about problems, he assumed we were in good shape. Because he did not know what was happening with the committee members, there was no way he could protect me in the defense.

I can imagine what the witnesses must have felt like in the O.J. Simpson trial. The questions were relentless, directive, and intended to test not only my academic competence but my stamina and courage. It was clear that a few members on my committee were out to see what I was made of. They even said it at the end, and commended me for my poise and professionalism under fire. One professor had six pages back and front of written comments and questions that neither my major professor nor I had any clue were coming. This lack of information about what to expect should never happen in a dissertation defense if possible. Though I passed and my committee members congratulated me on an excellent defense, I left there feeling wounded and mangled. I had friends waiting to celebrate but I just couldn't show. I don't think you should have to break somebody down just to see if he or she can win. Unfortunately this is the story of too many doctoral candidates, black and white.

One of the best things you can do is to talk to other students about the process and attend dissertation defenses in your department. Most colleges and universities post listings of doctoral dissertation defenses and they are usually open to the public. At least 6 months to a year before your defense is scheduled, start going to defenses in which the committees are made up of some of the same people who will be on your committee. Not only will this give you a feel for how the defense should be conducted, but it will also let you see your committee members in action. Take notes about their style of questioning, their demeanor, and what their goal seems to be in influencing the defense. The person you see in the dissertation defense may or may not be the person you know from the classroom or special project. The dissertation defense is a different animal, and these folks are serving as a panel of experts scrutinized by their colleagues with the responsibility for determining whether you have the credentials to get into this elite club. No matter how supportive your committee members may be, this is still the job they are assigned by the school and the field of study.

SPECIFIC TASKS FOR
ENSURING A GOOD DEFENSE

Prepare a formal discussion of your research to be presented for about the first 30 minutes of your defense. Make it spectacular and professional, using whatever audiovisual aids that are appropriate and available. Your goal is to impress your committee and "blow them away" from the very beginning. This presentation is a speech to be rendered with fact and charisma. Plan what you are going to say and practice it. Make simple, organized, and aesthetically attractive notes to take with you into the defense. Though your content and research may be good, it is a major turnoff if you are disorganized and your materials lack professionalism. If you are going to use overhead projections or slides, have them computer-generated and professionally mounted. The same goes for charts and graphs to be handed out. By using brief charts and graphs of results, you can nail the major points that you identified in your research. Because you have the opportunity to control this part of the defense and the questioning to follow may get rocky, you want to establish your poise, competency, and ability right here and right now. You cannot afford a weak opening presentation.

Besides discussing your methodology, findings, and the other technical aspects of your work in the opening statement, be sure to talk about your interest in the subject and the impact that you hope your research will make. The stronger the impact, the better. Identify many of the potential questions that you think may be asked and include them in the discussion. Be aggressive. Don't be afraid to talk up front about the weaknesses in your research. Don't tear your own paper apart, but acknowledge areas for improvement and offer potential solutions.

Anticipate some actual questions that you think you will be asked. Prepare and practice the answers. Ask your major professor for a list of potential questions. Ask your committee members, if appropriate, for a list of questions. Ask other doctoral candidates for questions because many questions about methodology and statistical analysis are fairly standard. Most important, if you realize that there is some technical information that you do not understand, particularly relating to the methodology and statistical analysis, get help from an expert. If you do not understand what you did or why you did it well enough to reasonably explain it, usually you will not pass the dissertation defense. Not only will the committee ask you about techniques you did use, they will also want to know why you eliminated the ones you didn't use. For most, this is the most intimidating part of the defense.

Not every dissertation defense is a harrowing experience. Many people have said that it was a wonderful opportunity to discuss their research in a supportive, empowering environment. I sincerely hope that yours is that way. Nevertheless, meanwhile I recommend that you get prepared, because almost everyone says that the confidence from knowing your stuff is more than half the ammunition needed for the defense.

GETTING THE REST OF YOU
TOGETHER FOR THE DEFENSE

Now that you are intellectually prepared, what else should you do?
First, attend to tapping your inner power. How do you go to that
special place inside you that has power, strength, and courage? Many
do it through prayer, meditation, reflection, or other methods. One
of the methods most widely used by athletes and others is commonly
called using affirmations. Psychologists have demonstrated that repe-
tition is extremely important in changing our thinking about ourselves
and influencing our confidence and sense of invincibility. Using affirmations is simply the art of repeating over and over positive thoughts
about ourselves that eventually become etched in our subconscious
minds, not just as statements at the conscious level. Interestingly
enough, we repeat negative things about ourselves all the time without
giving it a thought. If, for example, we keep saying to ourselves that
we are too ugly, or too short, or too fat, or too skinny, it won't be long
before we believe it. Just as this negative self-talk works on our
thinking, so can positive self-talk. Changing our self-talk is particularly
important for African Americans. We've heard so much about who we
are from so many people and a great deal of it has been negative. We
are still in the process of retelling our stories and "scripting" what will
become our new personal and cultural histories. Much of the "how"
we attain this goal will be through mass accomplishments in fields and
activities once felt to be attainable only by other ethnic groups. These
mass accomplishments will only be made by people who believe that
they can.

Students going through the process at the predominantly white
university where I teach often ask me how I was and still am able to
maintain my sanity in the face of sometimes troubled waters. Before I
ever get to the part about the mechanics of being a good scholar, I always
talk about learning who you are and believing in yourself. This is really
the key because most people of average intelligence with the appropriate
discipline can get through the academic exercises as long as they don't
give up. Case in point, and mentioned earlier, at least 50% of African
American doctoral candidates who are ABD (all but the dissertation)
never finish the degree. At most schools, ABD means that students have
completed all of the course work and passed the comprehensive exams.

Many of these students have even done a significant amount of work on the dissertation, but they never finish. They just give up.

There is a statement heard quite often in our communities that says African Americans have to work twice as hard to prove themselves brilliant and competent. Generally, I believe this. When I was much younger, I only understood this in literal terms, and I really didn't believe it. An "A" on an exam was an "A." I busted the exam and studied a lot less than most of my white counterparts. So, I didn't get this twice-as-hard thing. What I didn't realize at the time was that I wasn't proving myself to the exam; the exam was an inanimate object. What I now realize is each day, no matter how routine, is a proving ground where I have to prove myself repeatedly to people who are not inanimate objects and have biases and opinions. Many of these people choose not to look at the facts about who we are, because if they did there would be no question about the merit of our existence as equals.

In the face of difficulty, stay centered on who you are. Never forget that you already have all of the power that you need to succeed. Remember, affirmations and positive self-talk repeated over and over help to convince us that we can do it even if we don't believe it when we start. Said often enough, anything becomes believable. Make your own affirmations or use those of others. Say them every day, especially when fear and anxiety pop up. You are not alone but in the company of countless athletes and other successful people who use positive self-talk to bolster their confidence and belief in themselves.

Here is a list of affirmations geared for the dissertation defense.

1. Without a doubt, I'm ready for the defense.

2. I will sail through this defense with confidence and ease.

3. I am supported and respected by the members of my committee.

4. I am here to "kick some butt" on this defense.

5. I'm good and I'm here to let you know.

Affirmations should reflect what you want to be the outcome of your focus. Your goal is to pass, but you don't want to *walk in* and be *carried out* on a stretcher. So, when you are making your affirmations, don't just say such things as "I'm going to pass this defense" or "no matter what, I'm going to make it." Proclaim that this will be done with ease or that you will sail through the defense. Don't fill your head with thoughts that this is going to be hard and I'm going to have to struggle through. It may be hard, but you don't have to struggle through. See it as a race to be won and affirm that you are the Michael Johnson, Gail Devers, Gwen Torrence, or Donovan Bailey. Instead of sprinting to the finish line as poetry in motion, many a student has walked out of that room after the defense looking as if they just won the Kentucky Derby (rode hard and put up muddy). And that, my friends, is not a pretty sight for black folks.

OTHER PRACTICAL PREPARATIONS

Get yourself organized so that you can start the day of your defense at peace, with ease, and without chaos. Get a good night's rest the night before the defense. Staying up all night doing last-minute cramming is not a good strategy for the defense no matter how many times it has helped you ace exams. You are working from a different principle here. If you focus on the prep pointers mentioned earlier in the chapter, you will be academically ready for the defense. That's not the primary issue on the day of the defense. Staying up the night before memorizing minute facts about your dissertation results won't help you much. But, a good night's rest will. Remember, the defense is about stamina. It's about being sharp, able to think on your feet, in control of your emotions. These qualities are much more difficult to call up if you are running on sleep deprivation.

Beginning at 5:00 P.M. the evening before the defense, all preparations should cease except the use of affirmations and one final review of your presentation notes the morning of the defense. You should be ready for the defense at least 24 hours before it is scheduled. On the night before, pack your briefcase and organize your materials so that all you have to do is pick them up and go. They should be so impeccably organized that once you arrive at the defense you take them out and begin; no shuffling, arranging, and so forth. Eat a healthy meal, preferably one paid for by someone else. This always makes you feel better. Just make sure it's someone who supports you to the max and knows all the right things to say. Take in a funny movie. Check in with friends and family. Say your prayers or do whatever it is that you do to tap into your inner power. Go to bed at a decent hour. Even if you can't sleep, get in bed so that your body will know that it should be in the relaxed mode although your mind may be telling it something different. While in bed, listen to soft jazz with guitar and piano, drink herbal tea, read a Terry McMillan novel—the idea is to relax.

Now for a more touchy subject, let's talk about what to wear. Consider this a job interview at the White House. What would you wear if you really expected, hoped, or whatever to get the job? Casual won't work there. It's interesting that when people of color wear casual clothing to events as important as these, it seems to make them appear unconcerned, less competent or less commanding. Equally as important, don't disrespect your African American professors in an afrocentric college or university by showing up for your defense in casual clothing. No matter how modernized and liberated we think we have become, standard business attire is still an integral part of making that impression. I know that there will be many of you who think I'm off base with this advice, but look at the movers and shakers in *Black Enterprise Magazine* or look at pictures of Johnnetta Cole, former president of Spelman College, when she's out doing business and you'll see what I'm talking about. How you look still affects what people think about you. As bizarre as it may seem, I know people who have done a good job on their dissertation but did not handle themselves well and failed their defense only to have to suffer through it again. Conversely, I know other people who had weak areas in their papers but because they gave remarkable performances at the defense passed with minimal revisions. Remember, impression is half the battle and your goal is to blow them away in the defense so this thing can be over.

Other common sense tips about what to wear to avoid being a fashion faux pas include the following:

1. Make sure that your outfit is appropriate for the occasion. Business attire works well. A dress may be a nice thought, but not any dress will do. For example, avoid the "nighttime look." Suits and ties are still appropriate and impressive.

2. Make sure you know that what you are wearing looks good on you. Get in front of the mirror and "strut your stuff." Remember when James Brown said, "I look so good I could slap myself." That's the look you are going for. You want to feel powerful, not self-conscious because you don't like the way you look.

3. Go light on the makeup, strong with the power hair attack. But, do leave off your name cut into the back of your fade for this event.

4. For sisters *and* brothers, get your nails manicured so that when you are "giving it to 'em," your hands are impeccable.

5. Make sure your clothes are spotless and well-pressed. Don't wear that shirt one more time if you know that ring around the collar has turned into that lane around the interstate. The rest of the shirt may

be clean and pressed, but what will stand out is the ring around your collar. If you don't iron, send it to the cleaners or beg someone to iron it for you. All black folks in my generation used to iron until white folks taught us that if you put it on right out of the dryer, you can wear it.

6. Last, but not least, polish your shoes and get a decent briefcase to carry your stuff in.

WHAT TO EXPECT AT THE DEFENSE

First, be on time and be ready. Ask your calmest friend to accompany you or meet you at the location of the defense about the time you think it will be over. Even if your major professor and/or your committee is taking you out after the defense, you want to contact someone from your personal support system. It's interesting that most people's spouses or significant others say they "can't take" the defense. So, if that's the case, let them wait outside.

Be poised, confident, and pleasant. Commonly, everyone will meet in the room to exchange greetings and your major professor will outline the process for the defense. Then, expect them to send you and any spectators out of the room while they discuss your dissertation. As far as I can tell, this seems to be a ritual for doctoral defenses. It would be more humane if they could get together 30 minutes before the scheduled time of the defense to get the discussions out of the way instead of having you sit outside the room approaching your anxiety threshold. And you know, the longer they take, the more worried you get, because something must be wrong. Don't let it rattle you. It's part of the initiation.

Make a dazzling presentation and settle in for the questioning. Imagine that you already are a brilliant researcher and you are answering questions from colleagues or the press. Don't see yourself as a second-class citizen who needs these five (or so) people to validate your worth. This is just your dissertation, not your life. Too many students think these two things are synonymous, and once that happens you have given up a great deal of your personal power; held hostage by the thought that if you don't succeed at this, life is over. I am learning to take the attitude and developing the faith to believe, "this or something better." Whenever I can come to peace with this idea, it always works out for the best with a minimum of stress and worry.

Once the questioning begins, focus on one question at a time. If you don't understand, ask them to repeat the question. Think carefully about the answer before you proceed. If you have answered the question to the best of your ability and your committee has moved on, you should move on in your mind as well. Don't become fixated on some answer that you have already given. If you have another thought about a particular question asked previously and you think it would be helpful, ask if you can briefly revisit that question, but keep these requests to a minimum. Don't be afraid to ask members of your committee their opinions about points made in your responses. Hammer home the pivotal ideas and results integral to your study.

Below are some frequently asked questions about trouble spots during the defense.

Q: What if you are asked a question that you have no clue about?

A: Make sure that you understand the question and if you still don't know, say you don't know, but remain calm and poised. Another strategy is to ask the person who asked the question what his or her thoughts are on the subject. Of course, tact and diplomacy are the keys here.

Q: What should you do if you get asked an absolutely stupid question?

A: Act as if the question is as important as any question you've ever heard and answer it as if your response is vital to world peace. Then, get home and tell all your friends and especially your doctoral colleagues what kinds of buffoons already have doctorates and have the nerve to try to give you a hard time.

Q: What should you do if one committee member becomes fixated on a line of questioning that is going nowhere?

A: Attempt to answer the question and at the first available opportunity shift the focus to another point in your response by engaging another committee member to express his or her views on your point. If this doesn't work, give your major professor "the eye" signaling him or her to jump in, as long as your major professor is not the one asking the question. If your major professor is the one asking the questions, give him or her the "you are dead" signal or feign a seizure.

Q: How should you handle a committee member who is obviously using your dissertation defense to settle a vendetta?

A: Don't get defensive. Remain calm, poised, and in control of your emotions. Answer each question as best you can without acknowledging the person's behavior. If you remain professional and detached, the committee member is the one who ends up looking like the fool.

Q: What should you do if your committee members carry on long, rambling conversations about your dissertation without including you?

A: Nothing. Just sit back and catch your breath.

Q: What should you do if you get totally rattled?

A: Ask for a break, splash cold water on your face, say an affirmation, and get back to the defense.

THE ULTIMATE DEFENSE PREP

My friend Sonya, a *young* (under 30), bright, articulate, attractive African American PhD tells a hilarious story about her preparation and what to expect at your dissertation defense. She swears the story is true, so I'm passing it on exactly the way she told it to me.

"I Was Ready to Wear Them Out"

All right!!! Okay!!! Okay!!! Okay!!! I've calmed down a little. . . . But, in approximately 1 hour I will be addressed as Dr. Anderson for the first time following the submission of my "almost" final draft and getting this oral defense over. I have no fear. Well, maybe a little nervous energy, for after all I'm about to go before the academic *Who's Who* of my department. No need to be scared today. I've practiced what I am going to say at least 100 times, and I've already had the sleepless nights, cold sweats, and hair coming out.

As I climb three flights of stairs in my purple leather pumps carrying a box full of drafts, one for each of the committee members (the above referenced academic *Who's Who*), I reflect and find unspeakable joy in the fact that all of this unnecessary madness and brutal intimidation will be over in a matter of minutes. My game plan for a successful and brief oral defense was in place and beyond the rigorous academic preparation, I had three major attack points.

1. Wear all purple (dress, panty hose, and shoes) with gold accessories. Rationale: The department chair and "top dog" is a member of the Omega Psi Phi Fraternity, Inc. He will appreciate the colors and become distracted.

2. Place all drafts in attractive, expensive, uniform binders. Rationale: Committee members will be impressed by the professionalism, extra effort, and will in turn give extra consideration.

3. Do not challenge any comments made by the esteemed professors. Do not even challenge the "wanna-bes" who simply pop in to assist the *Who's Who* in the art of intimidation. Remember, every comment is a good point and a good idea. Rationale: Empower them until they sign off and then take your own power.

Well, my All right, All right, All right turned into All Wrong. That was the quickest hour probably ever imagined and my well-oiled plan went up in smoke. The department chair, the man that I had adorned myself in purple for had left the school. No notice, no letter, no phone call, no nothing. The only notice I got was to be turned around at the door in my purple outfit having climbed three flights with that heavy box and told that my dissertation defense had been canceled. Come back in a month. You can imagine that I was devastated, pissed, and up to my neck in disbelief.

Once getting over the initial shock, I went back to the worry mode—new committee member and chair, new prep, and new sleepless nights and hair falling out. My defense eventually was rescheduled and I passed. But, the moral of the story is: Expect the unexpected, take it in stride, never give up, and do the right kind of prep!

WRAPPING UP THE DEFENSE

Once the questioning ends, graciously thank your committee for a lively discussion and expect to be sent out of the room again. This is when they discuss your performance in the defense and decide how they will proceed regarding your dissertation. This is another part of the process that produces high levels of anxiety because you know that they are deliberating. If there were some weak parts of your paper and defense, it's up to your major professor to try to negotiate on your behalf. As a rule, this is true, "the longer they deliberate, the more likely it is that they have not reached a consensus and you have problems." When a decision is made, you are brought in to receive the results.

Here are possible results.

* Pass without revisions: You passed the dissertation and the defense and they all signed it on the spot. There's nothing else for you to worry about except the technicalities of printing, binding, and so forth.

- Pass with revisions: The committee generally felt good about your work but has suggested some changes to be made in the final draft. Usually they will sign it but expect your major professor to ensure that the changes are made. Some committees will want to wait until the corrections are made before they will sign it. The most important thing here is that you don't have to go through another defense.
- Fail: The committee feels that there is still major work to be done on the dissertation. After suitable revisions, another defense is scheduled.
- Fail the Defense: In a few rare instances, a student may have done a good job on the dissertation but totally bombed the defense. A second, less formal defense usually is scheduled.

THE END

Whatever the results of the defense, quickly get mobilized and complete the required tasks. If your committee suggested revisions, make them as soon as possible. If they flunked your work, defense, or both, make an appointment immediately with your major professor and get busy with reorganizing. No matter how you may feel, don't put a lot of energy into being happy, angry, or depressed until that dissertation is on its way to the bindery.

Here are some additional pointers that you may find helpful. First, hire a word processor who has experience with dissertations to prepare the final version that will be bound and placed on display. Most universities have very stringent requirements about margins, fonts, headers, widows, orphans, and so forth. Unless you have patience and strong publication skills, get someone else to do it. Most graduate schools and academic departments have one or more experienced secretaries who help students (for a modest price!) with their dissertations. Of course, have them work from the version you word processed yourself. Have them basically take care of minute details and formatting requirements, not the grind of typing text. Second, don't be tempted to order 15 extra bound copies of your dissertation. Order a few copies for yourself and copies for your parents' and grandparents' coffee tables. More than this is a waste of money. The rest of your relatives and friends would probably look at a picture of your hooding more often than read your dissertation.

THE LAST DANCE

The fact of the matter is that the defense is the last big appearance and it is an important one. It is the chance to showcase your research and talk eloquently and decisively about what you have done. It's like the last dance or "walking the burning sands before you cross over" if you have ever pledged a fraternity or sorority. There is a way to take control of the process and do it with more ease and less trauma. Do the prep work to make yours a positive event to remember.

10

LOOKING BACK AND MOVING FORWARD

ACKNOWLEDGING YOUR ACCOMPLISHMENTS

To have completed a master's or doctoral degree means that you have done a great thing. This was no small feat. For a few, it may have seemed like a cakewalk. But, for most others, it required great amounts of time, energy, and perseverance. No matter which experience you identify with as you reflect on graduate school, the accomplishment of receiving a graduate degree is something to be proud of. It should be applauded and revered by you and others because of its significance. It is a positive achievement in a world of so many distressful things that affect people of color.

Even with its magnitude, the significance of the degree may not be as notable to younger students as it is to many African Americans receiving advanced degrees who are older adults with families and other financial and societal responsibilities. To juggle a job, school, family, civic duties, and personal life changes is a tremendous commitment and exemplifies human triumph. Any person who does that deserves many accolades. It may be months or even years before you realize the importance of this step in your journey toward self-evolution. Despite future directions, the graduate school experience provided the opportunity to learn many important lessons; lessons about organization, time management, self-expression, political maneuvering, adult learning, confidence, perseverance, and other important things.

One of the most important ways to celebrate your accomplishment is to attend the graduation ceremony. You would think that once having completed the degree, students would not miss the opportunity to participate in graduation, but this is not the case. Many graduate students do not attend their formal graduation ceremonies. Many students actually finish their degrees at different times during the year, relocate, and don't come back for graduation. Others don't see it as important. Some choose not to participate as a form of angry rebellion; some just want to "get the hell out."

Though I'm not one who believes that symbols are always necessary for expression, I do believe in the graduation ceremony as a useful symbol. Attending graduation will make a difference in your self-esteem and always give you something to reflect on when you may doubt your ability to succeed. First, it brings recognizable closure to the work that you have done, not just for you but for others as well. Second, it serves as a form of proof that you can do anything you set your mind to. Third, others may be inspired by your accomplishments to seek advanced education. Last, your family and friends can express their pride and gratitude for your achievement. Go to your graduation. Proudly receive your degree. Bring as many family and friends as you can.

SAYING THANKS

A very wise woman and mentor to many professionals in Atlanta, Georgia, Reverend Carmen Young, always says that a grateful heart is the key to great success in this life. Being thankful helps us to appreciate and value our accomplishments and the gifts given to us by the universe. If we truly cherish them, we don't misuse or fail to use them. We honor them and refine them, making us more valuable and attractive in whatever endeavors we choose to pursue.

The opportunity, resources, and support to receive a doctorate or master's degree are indeed phenomenal tributes to many who have gone before us and paved the way through blood, hard work, and tears. My grandmother, who dropped out of school to help her family and began cooking in white folks' kitchens at age eight, comes to mind. She often remarked that she was so small when she started that they had to put a stool in front of the stove for her to stand on so that she could reach the top to stir the pots. Cooking in white folks' kitchens became her livelihood, her profession, her way to help support her family. That job became the way she helped to send her daughter away from a small town in South Carolina to Virginia State College in Petersburg, Virginia. I never heard her complain. If she was bitter I never knew, and I never saw her hang her head because she was a cook still earning $35.00 a week in the 1970s. But, I know there was something inside her that always wanted more, because she encouraged me to get my education and be the best scholar that I could. When my mother, brother, and I spent time with my grandfather and her while my dad was away in Vietnam, Korea, or somewhere else, she always brought home books and magazines that white people had discarded. I was a voracious reader and read everything I could get my hands on. She fed me the same lunch that she made for her white family so that I could be "strong" and ride my bike uptown every day to the library for the summer reading club. By the way, I was usually the only black child there except for a few of my friends who occasionally came with me. This was in the mid- to late-1960s and although desegregation was officially on the books, it took a bit longer to sink in in parts of the deep south. Frankly, I think the only reason I was so welcomed there was because I was Zula's granddaughter and the wonderful librarian, Mrs. Gee, took such a keen interest in me.

Looking back, I know that my grandmother didn't mean *strong* just in the physical way but spiritually, mentally, and emotionally as well. I'm sure that as you think back on your pursuits, many people come to mind who helped pave the way for your dream. I can also fondly remember my white chemistry teacher who was the advisor for the Forensics Club, a high school public-speaking league. She saw great talent in me as a debater and extemporaneous speaker. She took me under her wing and worked with me at a time in history when clearly she could have chosen to work with white students, because that would have been more socially acceptable in the South. I am thankful that our paths crossed, because this was where I got my start in public speaking.

People like these made great sacrifices for African Americans to excel in higher learning. We owe them a great deal of gratitude. In Reverend Young's writing, and in our almost daily conversations, she encourages me to give thanks for the knowledge that I have, the work that I do, and for the joy and blessings it provides to the universe. She says that it is wonderful to know that you are providing a service to humanity, giving of your talents and the gifts given to you. Each person has been created with a special mission to give the world. It is that person's own special blueprint. When you discover what yours is, and you will, it is a pleasure, a joy to do it. It ceases to be work. It becomes an expression of love and others are benefited. Every day, I say a short mantra written by Rev. Carmen that goes like this: "I give thanks for my talents, abilities, and the right places to exercise them. I am excitedly grateful."

Completing a doctorate or a master's degree is no insignificant feat. It required many hours of hard work and perseverance. To hafe endured and won is something to be thankful for. Here's a suggested "thank you" list.

a. Say thanks to the universe for the opportunity and the vast array of resources that made your learning possible.

b. Thank your inner self for a job well done. This is extremely important for your self-esteem, because sometimes the process can do a lot to tear away at the self-image.

c. Say a special thanks to your immediate family and friends who supported you and put up with you through the process. There were many people who called me often to encourage me, who chewed me out when I got off course, who I'm sure prayed for my swiftest completion because I was getting on their nerves, and even brought me meals during the crunch time. You'll have these folks too, and don't ever forget them. When you finish, have a party and publicly recognize these people. Send cards, flowers, or personalized tokens. Engraved gifts, such as glasses or mugs, picture frames, or clocks are nice for this purpose. Do it as a "thank you" for their support. Don't wait until you get their graduation gift. Do it first.

d. Do something really extraordinary for that spouse or significant other who stood by you all the way through thick and thin. He or she deserves his or her own share of your now undivided attention. And for that spouse or significant other who wasn't there for you when times were hard, who selfishly demanded more of you than you had to give, and who was a general "ass," give him or her something special too. Send a bouquet of flowers and a nice card explaining that "your services are no longer necessary." This advice is particularly useful for people having received the doctorate and are now moving to a much higher income bracket.

e. Send appropriate tokens of appreciation to your major professor, committee, and other colleagues who supported your process. In some cases, wrought with extreme pain and suffering, a simple "Thanks for the memories, it's been real!" will do.

f. And most of all, show your gratitude by freely giving the world your talents.

HEALING THE HURTS

It is not uncommon for the graduate school experience to evoke pain in survivors, particularly when receiving the doctorate. Several articles have been written on postdoctoral depression and its effects. The effects often have been described as feelings of loss, anger, and ambivalence now that the dissertation is over. Many people also have reported that they have difficulty making the transition back to a normal life, now that they no longer have the dissertation, projects, or course work to fill their time. Other new doctorates can relate to feelings, such as the intense pressure and/or the pain that they felt, having gone through a grueling defense. One commonly heard statement is that many people don't pick up their dissertation again for a year or more after it is over. Even master's level students report feeling exhausted and numb for the first few months after receiving the degree.

The first step in developing a strategy for dealing with the depression or pain surrounding the graduate school experience is to acknowledge that the hurt does exist and seek to identify where it came from. Was it a particular professor, the dissertation drafts, or a culmination of several events that caused the pain? Then, the student must see the experience for what it was—just an experience, and begin to rebuild self-esteem, reestablish friendships, and consciously work to focus on the outcome of the graduate school effort rather than the process. This may take conversations with mentors, peers, or supportive friends and family members. It may help to write about it and to engage in other active steps. Sometimes, professional help may be necessary. Do whatever it takes to put it behind you and move on.

BEING AN ALUMNUS MEANS MORE THAN
JUST GRADUATING FROM A SCHOOL

If being an alumnus is more than just graduating from a school, just what does being an alumnus mean? It's interesting that the definition may vary depending on whether the school attended was a historically black institution or whether it was a majority white institution. The definition may also vary depending on the graduate's perception of the school's prestige or status.

For African Americans graduating from many of the majority white institutions, it may be easy to fade into the "graduate-only" consciousness, particularly if the school has had a long history of racial discrimination or unrest, the experience was unpleasant or uneventful, or no real bond was formed. Sometimes one just doesn't feel endeared enough to participate in the festivities of most alumni affairs. I myself felt the same way at first about the majority white institution that is my graduate alma mater. Though my experience had been predominantly positive, I didn't feel as if I shared the same things in common with the people who were avid alumni. I missed the spark that I feel when I hear my friends who have gone to historically black schools talk about going back for homecoming or going to the Georgia Dome for the Black College Football Showdown. Maybe I felt that I had no significance to or no real place in the history of the university I attended.

Since then, I've changed my attitude and I want to work on carving out a new definition of what alumnus means to me. It's important, not because I need a place to go for homecoming but because I need to open more doors and make a place for young African Americans who will study there after me. When more African Americans start feeling that we do belong, then we will.

One of the most enlightening experiences I've had was to witness Charlayne Hunter-Gault and the now late Dr. Hamilton Holmes, the two black students who first integrated the University of Georgia, return to the University of Georgia for the annual Hunter-Holmes Endowment Lecture. As I listened to them talk about what it was like to have angry students chanting racial slurs, burning crosses outside the dorm, and having to be escorted by police, I could sense the importance of the role that I have to play in the future history (oxymoron, but I'm trying to make a point) of that university. Ms. Hunter-Gault's book *In My Place* accurately signifies the new role that I want to create for myself as an alumnus.

There are some ideas that seem to deepen the definition of alumnus that Hunter-Gault, Holmes, and others have exemplified. An alumnus should be an advocate. An alumnus should be a champion. An alumnus should be a supporter. An alumnus should be a mentor. And most of all, an alumnus should be a bridge over which other African American students can access the opportunity to make a contribution to the larger society by receiving graduate degrees. To operationalize that, it means more than just getting the degree and getting out, leaving the school behind as a vague or not-so-vague chapter in a part of one's history. No matter whether the school is predominantly white or historically black, it means making sure that other African Americans have the same or a better opportunity to get a doctorate or master's degree.

Dr. Agnes Green, President-Elect of the Morehouse College School of Medicine National Alumni Association, has this to say about what being an alumnus means (personal communication, September 17, 1996).

> We all have a duty to ensure that the educational opportunities that were provided us are available in an even better way for the scholars that come after us. At the Morehouse School of Medicine, there is a very strong formal and informal association of alumni. We love our school and what it means to us. We will teach our children to love it too, regardless of their career paths. We will teach them to love it because of what it stands for. Members and graduates interact with each other collegially and many still maintain strong personal friendships, which aid in networking and career progression. As formal members of the Alumni Association, we make suggestions and have discussions about important issues affecting the school, community, and nation. As African Americans, our participation as alumni is mandatory, especially as we survey the changing political and economic times in this country.

LIFE AFTER GRADUATE SCHOOL

Now that the thesis has been turned in and the dissertation is bound, what's next? African American scholars should have a somewhat clear answer to that question even if they need to do some fine-tuning. They should have been preparing for it from the beginning of their graduate school program. It is disastrous to ask that question at the end of a graduate school career. Life after graduate school should be nothing less than working "the plan."

A constant theme that I find myself preaching to new African American graduate students is the importance of having a "master plan"—a plan that serves as a guide for how they will conduct their lives over the next 5 years. One year is too short, 3 years is a significant evaluation point, and 5 years is enough time to see goals and outcomes reach fruition. Even if the plan is continually being tinkered with throughout the implementation period, there must be a plan.

Students often do not realize that having a plan can significantly affect the quality of their graduate school experience because it can put their courses, papers, presentations, and internships all in perspective. Some of the most successful students that I have ever seen have been the ones who have come with a plan, and everything that they do is related to that overall plan. This plan has a high correlation with postgraduate success and the amount of time necessary to realize it.

One student who comes to mind had a dual focus on public policy and law. In all of her classes, even the required ones, she found a way to link her research papers to some aspect of public policy or the implementation of policy in the area of family and child's law. She also wrote a couple of publishable papers and made presentations at a few conferences. Because she knew she wanted to go to law school, she spent an hour each day the first year of her graduate school program preparing to take the LSAT (Law School Admission Test). She maintained an exemplary grade point average in graduate school and scored well on the LSAT. Several law schools were anxious to matriculate her into their programs and provide money. Her goal was to finish graduate school, go to law school, practice family and children law, and eventually become a family court judge. She even had some idea of where she wanted to practice law. There is no doubt that this student will, in all probability, accomplish everything that she has set out to do. Once you have the plan, it just becomes a matter of working the plan. Graduate school should be a tool that is used to work the plan.

As African Americans, we have to start early. We need plans constructed similar to the one I just talked about. Though the economic status may be changing for the better for many of us, we cannot afford to stand around until the end, trying to make up our minds what we are going to do. A lot of the good stuff will already be gone. Increasingly, there is a threat to affirmative action, which means that many opportunities will change into different formats, and a new landscape for doing business will appear. We have got to be ready.

Many master's level scholars will be making the decision about whether to go on to doctoral programs or to work. My advice is to assess the situation, and if one can go on to a doctoral program, do it. A question that often comes up is, "should one get some work experience first before going on?" A number of folks would argue yes, but because of the risk of losing so many potential young scholars who get caught in the maze of financial and family responsibilities and never go back, I say push forward now while you have the chance, and find a way to get some experience while you are earning the doctorate.

Some graduates will have the dream of going on to doctoral degrees but will have to go on to work. If so, the graduate should make sure that this dream is included in that "master plan." Make a primary commitment to working toward that goal. Never give up.

There is an art to achieving employment and career goals. The strategy and complexity of it belong in a separate volume on surviving graduate school, but there are a few points to be appropriately included as we bring closure to this discussion of life after graduate school.

• Figure out what you want to do in life and go for it. Accept no limitations; your life depends on it. The following books may be helpful in identifying, charting, and achieving success:

> *Do What You Love and the Money Will Follow*
> (Marsha Sinetar, 1993)
>
> *To Build the Life You Want, Create the Work You Love*
> (Marsha Sinetar, 1995)
>
> *The Laws of Success* (Napoleon Hill, 1900)
>
> *Think and Grow Rich, A Black Choice* (Dennis Kimbro, 1992)
>
> *Success Runs in Our Race* (George Fraser, 1996)
>
> *Days of Grace* (Arthur Ashe, 1994)
>
> *The Instant Millionaire* (Mark Fisher, 1991)

• Build on your strengths by doing the necessary research and always focusing on your personal and professional development. Set aside time and money for self-improvement. Make it a scientifically planned, evolutionary process. Let no one or nothing stand in the way of your unfolding.

• Market yourself exquisitely. If you don't know how, get help or purchase one of the many books out there on the subject. Spend the money to develop the image of yourself so that you look like you are worth a million dollars. Your résumé, portfolio, or both should be descriptive and professionally done. Have two "interview suits": outfits that you can put on, go to any setting, and leave a memorable impression—a positive one, I might add.

- Learn how to network. Sometimes, it's not what you know but whom you know. The Department of Labor statistics indicate that approximately four out of five jobs are obtained through personal contacts, referrals, or references.

- Keep abreast of what is going on in your field and be willing to see the sometimes unspoken potential in a position even though it does not seem like the optimal job. At the same time, always know that life is full of infinite possibilities that you can access.

- Stay positive, always remembering that your success is not yours alone but that of many who will follow in your footsteps.

SURVIVING GRADUATE SCHOOL IS LIKE ONE LEG OF THE BIG RELAY

Completing graduate school is worthy of huge praise. It is an important accomplishment integral to the professional success of many of us. It teaches enormous lessons and makes most of us better people. We owe thanks for making it through.

For as much as we can lift our heads in pride for our accomplishments, we cannot become so proud that we become blind and complacent to the world around us. We have an obligation to excel and to be happy doing whatever work it is that we love. We have the responsibility to become strong alumni and create opportunities for others. We must realize that graduate school is not the end of the journey but a stop along the way.

Dr. Lettie Lockhart, a colleague of mine, put it eloquently.

> I thought that once I completed my PhD at Florida State University, the struggle would be over. I received a quick, rude awakening when a white professor congratulated me on becoming the department's first affirmative action doctorate. Though I was at first angered by it, I immediately realized that I didn't have to fall prey to the comment because I knew that it was not true. My course work had been exemplary and I had an outstanding dissertation to show for the work that I had done.

Since that experience, I have continued to survive the rigor of academia by becoming published, promoted, and tenured. But, I have also learned that I am not just who I am as defined by my academic success. It is only one piece of the mosaic of who I am. My journey has already continued long past graduate school.

11

WHEN RACISM REARS ITS UGLY HEAD

With Donna Walter and L. Denise Edwards

African American graduate students are often caught off guard to the degree that racism can rear its ugly head. Bolman and Deal in *Reframing Organizations* (1991) described the characteristics of an organization as follows: Organizations are complex; organizations are surprising; organizations are deceptive; and organizations are ambiguous. Of all the characteristics listed when it comes to racism, the university is most of all surprising and deceptive.

Racism is a serious problem, and college and university campuses are not immune from its destructive effects. An interesting irony is that colleges and universities are supposed to be institutions of higher learning; but often behaviors on college and university campuses actually reflect a great deal of ignorance.

Webster defines *racism* as the practice of racial discrimination based on a doctrine or teaching without scientific support, which claims to find differences in character, intelligence, and so forth based on race and seeks to maintain the supposed superiority and purity of some one race. Racism in graduate school may be covert and subtle, for example, hidden and disguised as a professor's prerogative on how he or she grades. Racism also may be overt, such as when a professor continually refers to African Americans as "those people." Last, racism can be unintentional, such as when a student makes an offensive remark but truly does not know that it is offensive.

THE WHITE MAN'S BURDEN

One of the first racial academic issues that many African American students face at a predominantly white college or university is that of being perceived as academically inferior to the majority of other students in the program. No one is quite sure how this phenomenon occurs, but it seems that a certain percentage of the African American students selected for any given class are thought of as having been selected for a graduate school program because of affirmative action. In other words, because affirmative action exists, it is believed that a certain number of all the African American students admitted will have admissions indicators lower than white students admitted. Once matriculation has occurred, all of the African American students go through a validation process in which it seems that professors and students alike are trying to determine which students are in the "affirmative action seats," and which can be thought of as peers and scholars. If you are identified as an "affirmative action admission," then you become the "white man's burden." Because of that label, behaviors toward you may range from acting as if you are invisible, to ostracizing you, to embracing you as if it is their duty to help the "less fortunate." Neither of these behaviors, nor others that fall within the range of these categories, are respectful nor supportive of African American students.

For example, invisibility is a condition that almost all African American students are aware of, whether they experience it firsthand or they observe it. Certain students are known to exist on the class rolls. But, when the time comes to be included in study groups or to be selected for special projects, they "do not exist." In other instances, though they may contribute to classroom discussions and be involved in communities outside their graduate program, they are still invisible within their own school.

Equally devastating is being selected by white students and professors as one of the "good black students." They find you fascinating and feel the need to embrace you for all of the wrong reasons. The reasons may be guilt, piousness, or the fact that you are seen as a novelty, or your persona as "safe." The "safe persona" is one seen quite often when students are not too radical in dress or appearance, or not too radical in their political opinions or expectations but accommodating and likeable, because others are not forced to accept them within the context of their cultural identity.

COVERT RACISM AND ITS EFFECTS

Covert racism is particularly difficult to understand and combat because it is so subtle. Often it's hard to know whether the negative behavior is racist or whether the professor or student involved is busy, insensitive, or just has poor taste and bad manners. In this situation, it is the track record toward African Americans that counts. For example, a white student goes to a professor during office hours to discuss his or her class performance and the conversation shifts to the upcoming midterm examination. The student is provided a great deal of assistance and the student shares the information with several white classmates who then go and get additional information about the test from the professor. Having overheard this information, several African American students make appointments to discuss their performance with the professor. None of these conversations included any mention of the examination and focused on the importance of having good writing skills, although no writing assignments had been turned in and the professor had no knowledge of the students' writing abilities. This is covert racism.

Another example of covert racism at the larger departmental level may be when schools "set up African American students" to bear the responsibility for cultural diversity through a lack of support for Black History and other cultural programs and then force students of color to bear the brunt of the fallout when racial problems do arise. Then when racial problems occur, the African American students are expected to solve them or just ignore them. In other words, schools do just enough to look as if they are promoting racial equality and social justice to recruit African American students, but their actions don't have the strength of any real follow-through.

Also, there are instances when African American students know that certain professors and students are racist because of affiliations and organizations of which they are members, but there is nothing that can be done about it. Consider this: An African American student may not want to take a "nap on" (figuratively or literally) a professor who has a confederate flag license plate, almost has a seizure from enthusiasm when they play "Dixie" at a football game, and fondly talks about the black lady that raised him or her.

The burden of having to always be aware of racism and "on one's toes" while attempting to excel and make great personal and professional gains is a heavy one. In this regard, the supposed "white man's burden" seems minuscule.

OVERT RACISM IS STILL ALIVE

It seems ironic that only a few years before a new millennium we would still be talking about vicious, open racism in our country and on our college and university campuses, but it is still alive and well. And, not just in the South either. Racial slurs and stereotypical remarks are made all of the time in academic settings, maybe because of the illusion of freedom of ideas and expression. Nevertheless, does freedom of expression provide the authority to demean or maliciously malign someone because of his or her racial background? We think not.

Though we are approaching the year 2000, African American students are still sometimes excluded from study groups because of the color of their skin. Their opinions are not often seen as valid, yet ironically they are expected to speak for the entire race when called upon to offer these opinions. Professors still have conversations behind the backs of African American students about how ill-prepared they are for graduate school when there are many white students far less prepared academically and emotionally. And active, violent hate groups are still allowed to establish themselves and operate on campuses around the country. Overt racism is alive and well.

RACISM BY RIGHT OF IGNORANCE

It is important to note that there are some persons who engage in racist behavior out of sheer ignorance that their words and actions are offensive and demeaning. In some ways, it is even racist by itself when a person is in a graduate school environment, never having had a meaningful relationship with a person of another race. In these instances, education may be more in order than condemnation. Nevertheless, this leads to the emergence of another important issue. Whose responsibility is it to educate on issues of race and culture? Why does it seem that African American students and faculty always have to take on the commitment of educating larger communities? Whether we realize it or not, the extent to which we participate in this education is a choice.

RACISM AND CLASSISM THAT SEPARATES BROTHERS AND SISTERS

There has been considerable discussion over the years about whether some dark sides of our relationships with each other as African Americans and men and women should be put into print for the world to see. A candid discussion about graduate school would be less than comprehensive if this subject was not addressed.

There are many hurts still to be healed in the African American community about shades of blackness, Afrocentrism, hair texture, social standing, socioeconomic status, and even the proper sorority or fraternity to pledge. We have all been in situations in which behavior was exclusionary even among African Americans because of some of these things. This problem may be even more profound for international students of color.

This form of racism and classism is significantly more devastating than that imposed by those of other races. This behavior symbolizes personal and cultural betrayal. The number of African Americans in graduate school settings is too small to be further subdivided. It is not mandatory that every African American student has to seek the close friendship of every other person of color. But what is mandatory is that African American students seek to accept, support, and empower each other despite individual differences. We cannot expect to get ahead by employing the same tactics of degradation and cultural castration.

RACISM AS INTERNAL AND EXTERNAL POISON

Racism is extremely dangerous for African American graduate students and scholars. It robs them of self-esteem and forces concentrated effort on the continual validation of their worth. It requires that great amounts of time and energy be invested in the pursuit of basic human rights granted others without question. Racism in the graduate school environment takes away the opportunity for students to immerse themselves in the thrill of learning. Learning does come but at a tremendously high price. Racism makes cynics of bright young stars waiting to make their contribution to the world.

As a culture and as people, African Americans can ill afford to have the visions of a generation of researchers, scholars, dreamers, and movers snuffed out by the effects of racism. Nor do we have the time to miss out on the tools necessary to actualize the vision. This is economic, social, moral, and emotional genocide for our communities.

WHEN AND HOW DO WE COMBAT RACISM?

There is an extensive process required for deciding when and if to combat racism. One must first decide in any given situation whether a particular battle is worth fighting. What are the real and human costs involved and what are the perceived benefits? What is the likelihood that the benefits can and will actually be received? Does one let a worn-out bigot of a professor live out his or her last days and die in ignorance, or is this a battle to be fought? Should we invest our time and energy here or invest our energy in making sure that a younger racist professor not get tenure at a particular institution or that a promising African American professor does? Is it worth it to correct a racist student each time he or she opens his or her mouth, or do we get up and walk out of a class in protest of his or her continually demeaning behavior and send a message that we will no longer entertain such nonsense? Do we handle racially related matters as a group or individually, even if the comment was made only to one of us?

These are important and pivotal questions that must be handled on a case by case basis. Each individual should be capable of defining his or her own level of tolerance, which can then be translated to a group norm. The only way for African American students to answer these questions is to talk about them openly and intelligently, weighing the costs and benefits of each battle looking to "right small injustices" but, most important, to change the landscape of the bigger picture.

One way to maximize the kind of communication necessary to help with the decision-making process is to develop relationships with African American professors who can serve as guides and sounding boards. Learn their styles, personalities, and the best way to communicate with them. Include them in the thinking and talking about racism.

In almost every instance, it is appropriate to inform a person when he or she has made a racist or offensive remark. It may be appropriate to acknowledge it publicly or privately depending on the circumstance. If the person continues with intentional racist language or actions, then other measures may be necessary. Students may seek to have the behavior stopped through the Dean's office at the departmental level or through a university grievance process. Other avenues may include mediation, writing letters to the university paper, or organizing a unified boycott of a class. Again, the benefits and costs must be weighed in choosing a specific battle and the means through which it will be fought.

Nikki Giovanni's book *Racism 101* (1994), gives some fundamental advice to the African American scholar that may help deter racism. Read the chapter on "Campus Racism 101." Do as Ms. Giovanni recommends. Be on time for classes, internships, seminars, or any other academic endeavors. Turn in assignments before or at the time that they are due. Proofread everything that you submit. Check for grammar, spelling, synthesis, and content. If you are having problems writing, attend workshops to improve your skills. These workshops are usually available for free on most campuses. Another piece of advice, be courteous to your professors. Call if you will be late or will miss a class. If you are a graduate assistant, perform your duties efficiently and conscientiously as if it were real employment, because it is. The professors whom you work for may serve as employment references in the future and may recommend you now for additional funding or other benefits based on your performance. Simply put, be the best that you can so as not to provide any excuse for a racist to justify his or her actions.

African American graduate students can also combat racism by developing mentor relationships with African American faculty members. Relationships can be developed with sincere faculty members of other ethnic backgrounds as well. There is strength in numbers. A strong showing of unity between students and faculty can be significant in sending a message that racism will not be tolerated. Illuminate unity by respecting and supporting African American faculty and other African American students. Don't engage in conversations that may appear not supportive and divisive. Even if you have a concern, go to that person directly and discuss it instead of engaging in destructive talk and actions.

Also, do not put African American professors in precarious positions by assuming that they will let you perform below required standards and submit substandard work. Strive to submit to our African American professors the very best of our scholastic efforts. Support African American faculty by attending their presentations and working with them on research and community projects. Form relationships with professors and students at other colleges and universities. Remember, there is strength in numbers.

African American students' knowledge of political events and processes also can assist in fighting racism. Stay informed and participate in university forums and other events that promote social justice and equality. Participate in policy-making activities as often as possible. Advocate on the state and federal level for equitable laws and programs. Organize letter-writing campaigns to legislators. Be active in community affairs, as private citizens may be helpful in advocating change on campuses.

On a personal level, the establishment of study groups and opportunities to interact socially can be very helpful in surviving environments where racism is present. Be there for each other, because for most graduate students, problems may go beyond academics and racism. Problems may run the gamut from separation, reconciliation, divorce, and dating, to major illness and death. Plan time to be together for fun. Go to the movies, eat out, go dancing, just hang out. Lean on your families and other support systems.

Equally important, do not isolate yourself from white classmates. It is not necessary to become a separatist just because you may attend a white university. If some social event connected with the school is being held, make sure that at least one African American student attends. In this way, you can keep up with what is going on and pass on the information to other black students. For instance, it was because of this type of socializing that we were able to find out that special arrangements had been made for a white student. She was allowed to make a substitution for a required class because she did not like the professor. This tidbit and others like it kept us in the know and empowered us to ask for what we needed from the school.

To combat racism, some African American students have found it helpful to believe in themselves and in a Higher Power that lets them know that they can succeed despite any adversity. Working on self-esteem should be a priority and a daily function. African American students must learn that even if they are deemed inferior by racists, this is not the truth about them. This must be a belief held close to the heart.

African American students must provide support for each other in environments that may not be set up to be supportive. As black students, we can share our stories of subtle snubs or the use of code words to describe black people in class. We know how it feels when a professor states that she deals with issues of cultural diversity only because she is being forced to by the university. We recognize the sighs and looks of exasperation made by white students and professors when we correct their assumptions about black people or ask them to look at an issue from a black perspective. We support each other through these and other incidents. In the words of one African American grad student, "If it wasn't for the group, I would have dropped out of this program a long time ago."

A PARTING PERSPECTIVE FOR MAKING A CASE ABOUT THE EXISTENCE AND EFFECTS OF RACISM ON AFRICAN AMERICAN SCHOLARS . . .

We cannot forget that racism does exist and often rears its ugly head in the graduate school environment despite all of academia's attempts at dissemination and applied understanding of the world's most complex ideas. When it does occur, we have choices about how we will think, feel, and act regarding ourselves and others. We can be burdened by the ignorance and small-mindedness of others or we can take calculated individual and collective action to rise above it.

The Students' Story

Just recently in a graduate program at a large university in the South, African American students were outraged by what many viewed as a derogatory memorandum "accidentally" circulated among faculty members and students. The memo was written by a member of the school's admissions committee to other committee members regarding the issue of affirmative action and admitting students of color over more qualified white applicants. Though the memo was for committee members only, it was intercepted via the fax machine and made available to several other persons. African American students felt hurt, enraged, and betrayed by the indication that this professor seemed to be a covert racist and because the comments may have been perceived as suggesting that current students were less qualified.

Tensions in the school were running high and there was the potential for a great deal of trouble, which may have affected not just the school and the administration but the students' education and quality of life as well. In addition to the African American students' outrage, white students were eagerly looking for the opportunity to jump on the reverse discrimination bandwagon, which may have affected graduate assistant-ships and other funding sources for students of color.

The African American students organized, consulted with mentors, and set up several meetings with the professor and the school's admin-istration. Ultimately feelings from both sides were aired, possible mis-understandings were addressed, inappropriate statements were acknowledged, and an apology was issued. In the end, many felt that the professor used poor skill in attempting to address an issue of importance to most graduate schools in light of the new legislation and court decisions on affirmative action. Most important, students stood up for what they believed in, and their voices were heard.

REFERENCES

Ashe, A. (1994). *Days of Grace.* New York: Ballantine.

Bolman, L., & Deal, T. (1997). *Reframing organizations.* San Francisco: Jossey Bass.

Cassidy, D. (1990). *The Graduate scholarship book.* New York: Prentice Hall.

Colgrove, M., Bloomfield, H., & McWilliams, P. (1991). *How to survive the loss of a love.* Los Angeles: Prelude.

Copage, E. (1995). *Black pearls journal.* New York: Morrow & Company.

Davis, G., & Parker, C. (1979). *Writing the doctoral dissertation.* New York: Barron's.

Ebony Magazine: Annual guide to college scholarships. Chicago: John G. Johnson Publishing Co.

Fisher, M. (1991). *The instant millionare.* San Rafael, CA: New World Library.

Fraser, G. (1996). *Success runs in our race.* New York: William Morrow.

Giovanni, N. (1994). *Racism 101.* New York: William Morrow.

Kimbro, D. (1992). *Think and grow rich, a black choice.* Westminster, MD: Fawcert.

King, B. L. (1995). *Transform your life.* New York: Anchor.

Leider, R., & Leider, A. (1989). *Don't miss out: The ambitious student's guide to financial aid.* Alexandria, VA: Octameron.

National Center for Education Statistics. (1995). *Digest of Education Statistics 1995.* Washington, DC: U.S. Department of Education, Office of Educational Research and Improvement, NCES 95-029.

Peterson's Guides. (1996). *Peterson's grants for graduate students.* Princeton, NJ: Author.

Peterson's Guides. (1997). *Peterson's guides to graduate and professional programs.* Princeton, NJ: Author.

Rossman, M. H. (1995). *Negotiating graduate school.* Thousand Oaks, CA: Sage.

Rudestam, K. E., & Newton, R. W. (1992). *Surviving your dissertation.* Newbury Park, CA: Sage.

Sinetar, M. (1995). *To build the life you want, create the work you love.* New York: St. Martin's.

Taylor, S. (1993). *In the spirit.* New York: Amistad.

Taylor, S. (1995). *Lessons in living.* New York: Doubleday.

VanZant, I. (1995). *Value in the valley.* New York: Simon & Schuster.

INDEX

ABOUT THE AUTHOR

Dr. Alicia R. Isaac currently resides in Stone Mountain, Georgia and is an Assistant Professor at the University of Georgia School of Social Work. She holds the B.A. degree in Behavioral Sciences from Erskine College, the Master of Social Work, and the Doctorate in Public Administration from the University of Georgia. Prior to serving as a faculty member, she was the Director of Masters Admissions for the University of Georgia School of Social Work for 5 years. The knowledge and expertise that Dr. Isaac shares in this book comes not only from her own experiences and the experiences of her colleagues, but from having guided the successful admission, matriculation, and graduation of many students.

In addition to her academic pursuits, she is very active in community service in the metro Atlanta area and believes in the power of believing in yourself. An avid golfer, she eventually hopes to establish a youth golf program that will teach young people the value of commitment, focus, self-discipline, positive thinking, having a dream, and never stopping until you reach your goals. Much like the formula for succeeding in graduate school.